young beginner's g

SHOOTING
&ARCHERY

tips for gun & bow

W.H. "CHIP" GROSS

Creative Publishing international

Minneapolis, Minnesota

W. H. "Chip" Gross has been a shooter and hunter all his life. As a certified hunter education instructor and shotgun shooting instructor for the Ohio Department of Natural Resources, Division of Wildlife, he taught thousands of young people and adults to shoot and hunt. He is the author of several outdoor books, and his writing and photographs have been published in a wide variety of outdoor magazines, such as *Wild Ohio* magazine, *Country Living, Women in the Outdoors,* and *Redfish Nation.* Chip and his wife, Jan, live near Fredericktown, Ohio.

Creative Publishing international

Copyright © 2009
Creative Publishing international, Inc.
400 First Avenue North, Suite 300
Minneapolis, MN 55401
1-800-328-3895
www.creativepub.com
All rights reserved

President/CEO: Ken Fund
VP for Sales & Marketing: Kevin Hamric
Publisher: Bryan Trandem
Acquisitions Editor: Barbara Harold
Editor: Jennifer Gehlhar
Production Managers: Laura Hokkanen,
Linda Halls

Creative Director: Michele Lanci-Altomare
Senior Design Managers: Brad Springer,
Jon Simpson
Design Manager: James Kegley
Cover & Book Design: Lois Stanfield
Page Layout: Lois Stanfield

Library of Congress
Cataloging-in-Publication Data
Gross, W. H. (Warren H.)
Young beginner's guide to shooting &
archery : tips for gun & bow /
W.H. "Chip" Gross.
 p. cm. -- (Complete hunter series)
 Includes index.
ISBN-13: 978-1-58923-409-3 (soft cover)
 ISBN-10: 1-58923-409-X (soft cover)
 1. Shooting. 2. Hunting guns. 3. Archery. I.
Title. II. Series.

SK274.5.G76 2008
799.2'0283--dc22
2008007060

Cover photograph © iStock Photo

Printed in China

10 9 8 7 6 5 4 3 2 1

CONTENTS

Rifles were named for the spiral grooves cut into the inside of their barrels, known as rifling.

INTRODUCTION

Whether you're punching holes in paper with a rifle or handgun, crushing clays with a shotgun, or shooting a bow and arrow, one word describes shooting: FUN! And the great thing about shooting is that you can do it for the rest of your life.

You've probably played some sports involving a ball—baseball, football, basketball, soccer, etc. As enjoyable as those sports are for you now, most people don't continue playing them throughout their lifetime. I know, because I've been there. When I was growing up I played them all: baseball in summer, football in fall, and basketball in winter. But during that same time, my father was teaching me to be a shooter and hunter. Of those five activities just mentioned, guess which ones I still do today? You're right, shooting and hunting. And I plan to continue doing them for as long as I live.

But as much fun as the shooting sports are, they require a higher level of responsibility than other sports. For example, if you throw a baseball the wrong way, kick a football or soccer ball the wrong way, or shoot a basketball the wrong way, will you cause major injuries? Probably not. The shooting sports are very different. If you handle a firearm or bow carelessly, the consequences can be irreversible. Always keep in mind that once you pull the trigger of a gun or release an arrow from a bow, that bullet or arrow can never be called back. Whatever damage is done, is done forever.

The good news is that you're ready to take on the responsibility that comes with shooting. Welcome to the shooting sports, activities that will continually challenge your skills and at the same time provide fun and satisfaction for a lifetime.

Shooting is a fun outdoor activity you can do your entire lifetime.

chapter 1

FIREARMS

If you have ever been to a large Fourth of July fireworks display, you were probably pretty impressed. Fireworks were discovered in China thousands of years ago when gunpowder was first developed. The Chinese used this gunpowder in long tubes to fire projectiles during times of war. As a result, the cannon was born, and handheld firearms—rifles, shotguns, and handguns—eventually followed.

RIFLES

Rifles were made to shoot one bullet at a time. They were developed for shooting stationary targets at long ranges, out to several hundred yards (meters). There are so many different rifles and they are used for so many different types of shooting and hunting that it is difficult to give standard descriptions. For example, a lightweight, single-shot .22 might weigh just a few pounds (kilograms), while a high-powered hunting rifle with a specialized target barrel might weigh 10 pounds (4.5 kg) or more. Most shooters or hunters using such a heavy hunting rifle would carry it on a sling over their shoulder, as the gun would be too heavy to carry in their hands for too long. On average, most rifles used for sport shooting and hunting weigh somewhere around 5 to 7 pounds (2.3 to 3.2 kg).

Barrel

Action   Stock

Rifles have three main parts: barrel, stock, and action.

How Rifles Got their Name

Rifles are named by caliber. Caliber is the diameter of the opening of the gun barrel. For example, if a rifle is .22 caliber, that means the barrel opening measures 22/100 inches in diameter (5.6 mm). Measuring in inches is the North American system of naming rifles; measuring in millimeters is the European system. Therefore, if a rifle is a 9mm, that simply means the barrel opening measures 9 millimeters in diameter (.36 inch). There are exceptions, and some rifle names can be a bit confusing. For instance, a .30/06 is a 30-caliber rifle that was first developed in the year 1906.

Remember to match the specific ammunition with the specific caliber of rifle you are shooting. Just because a rifle cartridge fits into the firing chamber of a rifle does not mean it can safely be fired in that rifle. The caliber designation of a rifle will be stamped into the metal on top of the outside of the barrel. Use only ammunition appropriate for that rifle. The caliber designation will also be printed on the box of ammunition.

Parts of a Rifle

There are three main parts to every rifle: barrel, action, and stock. The barrel is the long, metal tube the bullet travels down when the rifle is fired. The action is the part of a rifle that loads, fires, and unloads the gun. The stock is the part of the rifle that holds the barrel and action, and is usually made of wood or a synthetic material. You'll learn more about other parts of firearms later in this book, but for now just remember barrel, action, and stock. It will help you better understand how firearms work.

Barrel Rifling

Like early cannons, early shoulder guns (guns fired from the shoulder) were called smoothbores. In other words, if you looked down the inside of the barrel, it looked like a smooth tube or pipe. A gunsmith (someone who makes and repairs guns) eventually discovered that if spiral grooves were cut inside the metal barrel of a gun, the bullet would spin as it left the barrel, making the bullet fly more accurately. Those grooves cut in a barrel are known as rifling, and that's how the rifle got its name.

Spiral grooves cut into the metal on the inside of the barrel of a rifle spin the bullet, making it more stable in flight.

Here's how rifling works. Have you ever held a football by one of its ends and tried to throw it? You know what happens, the ball flies end over end and is not very accurate. But if you hold the football on its side, with your fingertips on the laces, what happens when you throw it? The football spins, becoming very accurate. It's the same with a rifle bullet. The rifling in the gun causes the bullet to spin as it travels down the barrel, making the bullet more stable in flight and ultimately more accurate.

Rifle Actions

Action refers to how rifles are loaded and fired, and how the empty cartridge case is ejected. A rifle has one of five actions: hinge, bolt, lever, pump, or semi-automatic. Some big-game hunting rifles are hinge actions, but they are not as common as the other five rifle actions. Hinge actions are more common in shotguns, so they will be covered in the shotgun section.

To open the action of a bolt-action rifle, a shooter must first raise the bolt and slide it back until it stops. To close the action, slide the bolt forward again and back down into its original position, locking the bolt in place. Some bolt-action rifles require that the safety button be pushed to the Off or Fire position before the bolt can be moved. If this is the case, remember to put the safety back to the On or Safe position once the bolt is in its closed position.

To open the action of a lever-action rifle, a lever (found on the underside of the gun) is moved downward until it stops. To close the action, move the lever back up to its original position.

To open the action of a pump-action rifle, depress the forearm-release button and pull the forearm (the front part of the stock under the barrel) back toward you until it stops. To close the action, move the forearm forward to its original position. It is not necessary to push the forearm-release button to release the forearm after the gun is fired, as it then releases automatically. This function allows for quick, successive shots if needed.

Shotguns are sometimes known as "smoothbores," because there is no rifling cut inside their barrels as with rifles and handguns.

To open the action of a semi-automatic rifle, pull the bolt back until it locks in place. To close the action, press the bolt-release button. This allows the bolt to slide back to its original position. Make sure your fingers are out of the way when you do this, as they could get pinched when the bolt slams shut. If a rifle has a cartridge(s) in its magazine, the opening and closing of the action will load a cartridge into the firing chamber of the barrel so that the gun is ready to fire.

Rifle Magazine

Ammunition used in a rifle is called a cartridge. A rifle magazine is where a gun holds the extra cartridges. Some rifle magazines are a tube under the barrel, while other magazines are built into the receiver (the receiver is the part of the gun action that receives the cartridge from the magazine). Either way, a magazine is simply where extra cartridges are held before being fired. Cartridges are normally loaded into a rifle's magazine by the shooter before being moved into the firing chamber by the gun's action.

Parts of a Rifle Cartridge

There are four parts to a rifle cartridge: case, primer, powder, and bullet. The metal case is what holds the other three parts of a cartridge together. The primer is the small, silver circle on the bottom of the cartridge. The gunpowder is inside the case. You can't see the gunpowder inside the case, but it's there. If you shake a cartridge, you can sometimes hear the powder moving inside. The bullet is at the front end of a cartridge, opposite the primer.

The cartridge described above is known as center-fire ammunition. That's because the firing pin of a rifle must strike the primer located in the center of the rear of the case to fire the cartridge. Some rifle ammunition, such as .22 caliber, is rimfire. That means the primer is enclosed inside the rim of the case. If a cartridge is rimfire, you won't see the primer.

How a Cartridge Fires

A rifle cartridge fires by a shooter first pulling the trigger of the gun. This sets in motion a quick series of events. The trigger releases a firing pin, which strikes the primer. The primer is a small explosive device that sends a small charge of fire into the gunpowder inside the case.

The gunpowder is instantly ignited by the exploding primer and burns very quickly. The burning gunpowder creates gases that expand and force the bullet from the case and down the rifle barrel.

When the bullet leaves the gun barrel, the gases escaping the end of the barrel are what you hear as the "bang" of a rifle firing.

Of course, all of this happens within a split second once the trigger is pulled.

Ammunition used in a rifle or handgun is called a cartridge (c, d, e), while ammunition for a shotgun is known as a shell (a, b).

Rifle Sights

Sights are used to accurately aim a rifle. There are three kinds of rifle sights used in most shooting sports and hunting: open, peep, and telescopic.

Open sights, also known as iron sights, have two parts: a front sight and a rear sight. The front sight is a small post, usually with a bead on top, located on the end of the rifle barrel. The rear sight is located farther back on the barrel and is either U-shaped or V-shaped. To aim the rifle, line up the bead on the front sight with the U or V in the rear sight, then line up the bead with the target.

Here's a shooting tip: Since the human eye can only focus on one object at a time, concentrate on the front sight when aiming. As a result, the rear sight and target will both be a little blurry, but by using this technique you will be more accurate in your shooting.

Peep sights are similar to open sights, except that a metal disk with a tiny hole in the middle replaces the rear sight. A shooter aims a rifle with peep sights by looking through the disk and then lining up the bead on the front sight with the target. Peep sights are used by many competition rifle shooters. They are seldom used in hunting because it takes more time to get on target with peep sights than open sights, time in which an animal could move out of range.

Sighting-in a rifle should be done from a firm rest, such as this shooting bench. Notice the pillow under the gun barrel to cushion it.

Telescopic sights are also known as scopes. When you look through a scope, you'll see two thin, intersecting lines called crosshairs. To aim a rifle with a scope, simply place the crosshairs on the target where you want the bullet to strike. Scopes magnify the target, but they also magnify any rifle movement made by the shooter. Telescopic sights are usually used for shooting long distances, such as big-game hunting. To be more accurate, a rifle with a scope should be fired from a solid rest.

An added safety tip when using a rifle, shotgun, handgun, or even a crossbow with a scoped sight is to never use the scope as a pair of binoculars. In other words, never look through the scope when scouting for game. A scope should only be used when actually aiming and firing.

Although not as common as the other three sighting systems, laser sights can also be used for aiming a rifle. Laser sights cast a light beam onto the target. If a rifle is sighted-in correctly, the bullet strikes where the laser light is placed on the target. Rifles equipped with laser sighting systems are not legal for hunting.

Chapter 3, Marksmanship & Shooting Fundamentals, will discuss how to "sight-in" a rifle properly.

Use the Safety!

Most rifles have a button on them known as a safety. When set to the "On" or "Safe" position, the safety blocks the trigger from being pulled. But safeties are mechanical devices that can fail. Never depend only on a gun's safety to prevent the rifle from firing. Always keep a safety in the "On" or "Safe" position until just before you are ready to fire a gun.

The safety on a rifle blocks the trigger from being pulled, but you should never count on a safety to prevent a gun from firing.

WANT TO EARN A SHOOTING PATCH?

The National Shooting Sports Foundation (NSSF) partners with USA Shooting to offer the Junior USA Shooting Team patch programs. The programs give young shooters the chance to earn an official riflery or shotgunning patch from the Junior USA Shooting Team, while at the same time learning safety and shooting basics. For more information, go online to http://www.nssf.org/JrUSA/.

SHOTGUNS

Shotguns were made to shoot many small pellets all at the same time. Shotguns are used for shooting clay targets or moving game at close range, usually out to about 40 yards (12 m).

Most modern shotguns weigh about 5 to 7 pounds (2.3 to 3.2 kg). This may not sound like much, but if you are not used to shooting shotguns they can seem heavy when you first pick them up. And a shotgun can eventually feel extremely heavy if you carry it around in the hunting field all day. With that thought in mind, a new or young shooter would probably do better to begin shooting with a slightly lighter shotgun than one that is too heavy.

How Shotguns Are Named

Shotguns are named by gauge. There are six common shotgun gauges: 10, 12, 16, 20, 28, and .410. Of those, 10-gauge is the largest shotgun and .410 the smallest.

Gauge measures the size of the opening in the muzzle of a shotgun barrel. Gauge is the number of lead balls, exactly the size of the diameter of the opening of a shotgun barrel, it takes to equal 1 pound (.45 kg). Here's an example: If it takes 10 lead balls with the same diameter as the opening of a shotgun barrel to equal 1 pound (.45 kg), that shotgun is called a 10-gauge. If it takes 12 lead balls with the same diameter as the opening of a shotgun barrel to equal 1 pound (.45 kg), that shotgun is called a 12-gauge. If it takes 20 lead balls with the same diameter as the opening of a shotgun barrel to equal 1 pound (.45 kg), that shotgun is called a 20-gauge. And so on.

Shooting a shotgun is very different from shooting a rifle or handgun; shotguns are pointed, rifles and handguns are aimed.

Basic shotgun shooting equipment—shooting glasses, hearing protection, shooting vest, and cap—need not be expensive.

The exception is the .410. The .410 is named by caliber like a rifle or handgun, not by gauge. In other words, the opening of the muzzle of a .410 shotgun measures $^{41}/_{100}$ of an inch (10.3 mm) in diameter.

Remember to match the same gauge shotgun ammunition with the same shotgun gauge you'll be shooting. How will you know for sure that you have the correct shot shell for the right shotgun? The gauge of a shotgun is stamped into the metal on the top of the outside of most shotgun barrels. It's then simply a matter of purchasing the correct ammunition for that particular shotgun. Boxes of shotgun ammunition are also marked by gauge.

Parts of a Shotgun

There are three main parts to every shotgun: barrel, action, and stock. The barrel is the long, metal tube the shot travels down when the shotgun is fired. The action is the part of a shotgun that loads, fires, and unloads the gun. The stock is the part of the shotgun that holds the barrel and action. You'll learn more about other parts of firearms later in this book, but for now just remember barrel, action, and stock. It will help you better understand how firearms work.

Barrel

Most shotgun barrels come in three standard lengths: 26, 28, and 30 inches (66, 71, and 76 cm). Some shotgun barrels are slightly longer or slightly shorter

Shotguns, like rifles, have three main parts: barrel, stock, and action.

than these lengths—for specialized hunting or shooting situations—but in general most shotgun shooters choose from one of the three standard barrel lengths. Their choice is based on what the gun will be used for most often. For example, most trapshooters and waterfowl hunters usually choose a 30-inch (76 cm) barrel for their shotguns, as the longer barrel helps them sustain a smooth swing and follow-through at the long-range targets they are usually shooting.

On the other hand, skeet shooters and small-game hunters usually choose a 26- or 28-inch (66 or 71 cm) shotgun barrel, because they are shooting clay targets or game at relatively short ranges. By shooting a shotgun with a shorter barrel, these shooters can get it swinging faster and can also use the gun more easily in confined spaces, such as when bird or rabbit hunting in dense brush.

When choosing a shotgun barrel length, keep in mind the old shotgunning adage that says, "What starts quick stops quick." What that means in practical terms is that a shotgun with a shorter barrel will start swinging quicker or faster than a shotgun with a longer barrel. The down side to the equation is that a short-barreled gun will also stop swinging more quickly. Follow-through is extremely important in shotgun shooting, so if a shooter stops his swing short, he'll miss the target. The choice of shotgun barrel length is up to the individual shooter. Just remember to match shotgun barrel length to the type of shooting or hunting you will be doing most.

Many early shotgun barrels, manufactured before the year 1900, were

Eye and hearing protection are critical to good shotgun shooting. Notice the tinted shooting glasses and foam ear plugs on this young lady.

made of alternating ribbons of iron and steel twisted and welded together. These Damascus barrels are "softer" than modern-day shotgun barrels made of rolled or drawn steel. Therefore, shotgun shells loaded with modern, smokeless powder should never be used in old shotguns. Doing so could cause the guns to explode. If you have a question about whether a shotgun is safe to fire with modern ammunition, check with a gunsmith. Never take a chance by simply pulling the trigger and hoping for the best.

Choke

In the rifle section, you learned that rifles have rifled barrels. In other words, grooves are cut into the metal on the inside of the barrel, causing the bullet to spin. This makes the bullet more stable in flight and ultimately more accurate. Shotgun barrels have no rifling. Why? Because it is not needed. The small pellets that shotguns shoot—known as shot—are round. Therefore, unlike a bullet that is oblong, if they turn over in flight it is not a problem, they are still accurate. Because shotguns have no rifling, they are sometimes called smoothbores.

Shotgun barrels do have a slight constriction or narrowing in the last few inches (centimeters) of the barrel, known as choke. This narrowing of a shotgun barrel controls the spread of the shot as it leaves the barrel. There are four common shotgun chokes: cylinder, improved cylinder, modified, and full.

Cylinder, also known as open choke, is no constriction of the barrel. It allows shot to spread very quickly as it travels downrange. Skeet shooters or hunters shooting game at very close ranges may use a shotgun with cylinder choke.

Improved-cylinder choke is a slight narrowing of the barrel, keeping shotgun pellets together a little longer than cylinder choke. Hunters shooting game out to about 30 yards (27.4 m) might use a shotgun with improved-cylinder choke.

Modified choke is even more of a constriction of a shotgun barrel, and is a good all-around choke for most types of hunting. A good choice for most shotguns that don't have interchangeable choke tubes would be a modified choke.

Empty shotshell cases can be reloaded to save on ammunition costs.

A good shotgunning stance is facing the target, with one foot slightly ahead of the other; remember to keep both eyes open.

Some shotguns are made specifically for trapshooting; notice the high-ventilated rib on this gun.

Full choke is the most constricted narrowing of a shotgun barrel. Trapshooters, turkey, and waterfowl hunters usually use full-choke shotguns, as these shooters are usually firing at targets at longer shotgunning distances, 40 yards (36.6 m) or more.

To picture what choke does in a shotgun barrel, think about the spray from a garden hose. Open up the nozzle of a hose and water comes out in a broad spray, similar to cylinder or improved-cylinder choke. Close down the nozzle and water comes out more in a stream, similar to modified or full choke. Shotgun shooters should match their shotgun's choke to the distances they will be shooting.

Keep in mind, too, that pellets fired from a full-choke shotgun barrel will not travel any farther than pellets fired from a cylinder-choke shotgun barrel. The full-choke pellets will simply be more concentrated (stay together longer) farther downrange. Most modern shotguns come equipped with screw-in choke tubes, allowing a shooter to change chokes for various shooting or hunting situations. A shotgun equipped with choke tubes should never be fired without one of the tubes in place. Doing so could damage the metal threads where the choke tube screws into the barrel.

Shotgun Actions

There are four common shotgun actions: hinge, pump, bolt, and semi-automatic. The action of a shotgun loads, fires, and unloads the gun. There are also some lever-action shotguns, but that shotgun action is not as common as the other four.

To open the action of a hinge-action shotgun, the shooter pushes a small lever on the top of the gun. This allows the shotgun to "break" or hinge open. Hinge-action shotguns can be either single-barrel or double-barrel. If double-barrel, the barrels may be beside each other (known as a side-by-side shotgun) or stacked on top of each other (known as an over and under shotgun).

To open the action of a pump-action shotgun, depress the forearm release button and pull the forearm (the front part of the stock under the barrel) back toward you until it stops. To close the action, move the forearm forward to its original position. It is not necessary to push the forearm-release button to release the forearm after the gun is fired, as it then releases automatically. This function allows for quick, successive shots if needed.

To open the action of a bolt-action shotgun, raise the bolt and slide it back until it stops. To close the action, slide the bolt forward again and back down into its original position, locking the bolt in place. Some bolt-action shotguns require that the safety button be pushed to the "Off" or "Fire" position before the bolt can be moved. If this is the case, remember to put the safety back to the "On" or "Safe" position once the bolt is in its closed position.

To open the action of a semi-automatic shotgun, pull the bolt back until it locks in place. To close the action, press the bolt-release button. This allows the bolt to slide back to its original position. Make sure your fingers are out of the way when you do this, as they could get pinched when the bolt slams shut.

One other point about shotgun actions: If a shotgun has one or more shells in its magazine, the opening and closing of the action loads a shell into the firing chamber of the barrel so that the gun is ready to fire.

Make sure your cheek stays in contact with the top of the gun stock when shotgun shooting. This shooter is firing a hinge-action shotgun.

Shotgun Magazine

Ammunition used in a shotgun is called a shell. A shotgun magazine is where a gun holds the extra shells. Some shotgun magazines are a tube under the barrel, while other magazines are built into the receiver. Either way, a magazine is simply where extra shells are held before being fired. Shells are normally loaded into a shotgun's magazine by the shooter before being moved into the firing chamber by the gun's action.

Most shotgun shells measure 2¾ inches (7 cm) in length. That's the standard length for most gauges, but some shotguns can shoot 3-inch (7.6 cm) or even 3½-inch (8.9 cm) long shotgun shells. Make sure you know what length shotgun shell your shotgun can safely shoot. And just as with the gauge designation, the length of the shell that is safe to shoot in a particular shotgun will be stamped into the metal on the top of the rear of the barrel. It will say something like, "Use only 2¾-inch (7 cm) or shorter shells."

Always keep the muzzle pointed in a safe direction when loading and unloading a shotgun.

But keep in mind that a 3-inch (7.6 cm) shotgun shell will fit into a shotgun with a 2¾-inch (7 cm) firing chamber. The 2¾-inch (7 cm) chamber is really 3 inches (7.6 cm) long. Why? It needs to be because when a 2¾-inch (7 cm) shot shell is fired, the crimp on the end of the shell must open ¼ inch (.6 cm) to release the shot.

Again, a 3-inch (7.6 cm) shotgun shell will fit into a shotgun with a 2¾-inch (7 cm) firing chamber. But what will happen when the gun is fired? The barrel may explode, because the crimp on the end of the 3-inch (7.6 cm) shell has no place in which to open. This is a very important point and one that must never be forgotten: Use only the proper length shotgun shell for the shotgun you are shooting.

Parts of a Shotgun Shell

Shotgun shells have the same four parts as a rifle cartridge—case, primer, powder, bullet—plus one additional, a wad. A wad is necessary in a shot shell for two reasons: It seals the gunpowder, allowing it to burn faster, and helps cushion the shot as it travels down the shotgun barrel. Were it not for the plastic sleeves on a wad, some of the shot would scrape against the inside of the shotgun barrel as it travels toward the muzzle and become deformed or out of round. If that happens, those particular pieces of shot—known as fliers—are likely to fly out of the shot pattern and not hit the intended target.

The four parts of a shotgun shell are held together by the case. A shot shell case is usually made of plastic with a metal base. Most shot shell cases are color coded to prevent putting the wrong shell in a gun. For instance, most 12-gauge shells are either red or green and 20-gauge shells are yellow. Most 16-gauge shot shells are purple. But not all ammunition manufacturers follow this color-coding system for their shotgun shells, so make sure you have the correct gauge shell for the correct gauge shotgun.

The primer on a shotgun shell is the small, silver circle on the bottom of the shell. The gunpowder is inside the case. On top of the gunpowder inside the case is the wad, and on top of the wad is the shot. The top of a shotgun shell is folded over or "crimped" to hold it closed until being fired.

Double-barrel shotguns can either be over and unders (pictured) or side by sides.

Ammunition used in a shotgun is called a shot shell.

Sizes & Kinds of Shot

Not all shotgun pellets are the same size. For instance, size 00 buck shot is the size of a small marble. Nine of them fit into one 12-gauge shot shell. By contrast, size 9 shot is smaller than a pellet from a BB gun, and several hundred fit in a 12-gauge shot shell. The pellet size needed depends on the type of shooting.

Shot shell pellets are made from a variety of materials. Years ago, most pellets were made of lead. Today, because of environmental concerns, there are additional types of shot available, such as steel, bismuth, and tungsten. All waterfowl hunters must use nontoxic shot to prevent lead

Double-barrel shotguns give a shooter/hunter the option of a different choke in each barrel.

poisoning in water birds. Some public lands require hunters to use nontoxic shot while hunting all game, not just waterfowl. It is often unlawful to even carry shotgun shells containing lead pellets.

How a Shot Shell Fires

Pulling the trigger of a shotgun sets in motion a very quick series of events. The trigger releases a firing pin, which strikes the primer. The primer is a small explosive device that sends fire to the gunpowder inside the case. The gunpowder is instantly ignited by the primer and burns very quickly. The burning gunpowder creates gases that expand and force the wad against the shot, pushing both the wad and shot from the case and down the shotgun barrel. The gases escaping the end of the barrel make the "bang" sound. All of this happens within a split second once you pull the trigger. The shot travels toward the target, while the wad falls to the ground.

Unlike rifles and handguns, shotguns are not aimed, but pointed and fired quickly. Shotgun sights are very different than rifles or handguns. Most shotguns have a small bead on the barrel's top end, and no rear sight; some have a flattened "rib" down the top of the barrel. If "ventilated" (having slots

Shotgun shells (shot shells) have five parts: case, primer, powder, wad, and shot.

cut beneath it at regular intervals), a rib helps disperse heat from a shotgun barrel. If you shoot a lot of shells over a short period of time—as clay target shooters do—a rib helps you see the target better because of less heatwave distortion. A ribbed shotgun barrel also "dresses up" a shotgun more than a plain, round barrel.

Hunters sometimes add open sights or a telescopic sight to a shotgun when shooting deer slugs for big game. A deer slug is a single projectile fired from a shotgun. Rifling a slug makes it spin as it travels down the shotgun barrel. Rifled-slug barrels can also be purchased for shotguns. These specialized barrels, usually used for deer hunting, come equipped with open sights. Safety tip: When using a gun with a scoped sight, never look through the scope when scouting for game. A scope should only be used when actually aiming and firing.

Use the Safety!

Most shotguns have a button on them known as a safety. The safety blocks the trigger from being pulled, preventing the gun from firing. Never depend only on a shotgun's safety to prevent the gun from firing. Always keep a safety in the "On" or "Safe" position until just before you are ready to fire a gun.

Shotguns can be fired from a sitting position, which is often the case when wild turkey hunting.

Shooting a handgun with a two-handed grip rather than one-handed makes the gun more stable and your shots more accurate.

HANDGUNS

Handguns, such as pistols and revolvers, are more like rifles than shotguns because they have rifling in the barrel; but because of their short length (generally less than a foot long) and light weight (only a pound or two), handguns are more dangerous. A careless twist of your wrist and you will be pointing a handgun in an unsafe direction. Handguns are not for beginning shooters. Handle and fire your first handgun under the instruction and supervision of an experienced adult.

How Handguns & Handgun Ammunition Are Named

Handguns and their ammunition are named by caliber, similar to rifles. Handguns shoot either center-fire or rimfire ammunition. The ammunition used in a handgun is known as a cartridge.

Parts of a Handgun

Handguns have the same three main parts as a rifle or shotgun: barrel, action, and stock. However the stock of a handgun is called the "grip," not the stock. Most handgun grips are replaceable, so if you don't like the feel of a certain grip—too large or too small for your hands—it can be replaced. The barrel of a handgun is the metal tube the bullet travels down when the gun is fired. The action is the part of the handgun that loads, fires, and unloads the empty cartridge case from the gun.

Handgun Actions

There are four common handgun actions: revolver, semi-automatic, bolt, and hinge. A revolver holds the cartridges in a cylinder that turns or revolves as the gun fires. Revolvers are either fired single-action, double-action, or both. To fire a single-action, pull back the hammer with your thumb until it locks in place. This is called cocking the revolver. Pull the trigger to fire. Most of the handguns used in the late 1800s were single-action revolvers. Revolvers that are more modern can be fired single-action and double-action. To fire a double- action, simply pull the trigger. The gun cocks itself, then fires.

To load or unload a revolver, push the latch on the side of the gun. The cylinder will swing out. If the revolver cylinder remains in place, you must load or unload through a loading gate on the side of the handgun.

The cartridges in a semi-automatic handgun are stored in a magazine that slides in and out of the grip of the gun. Like most revolvers, semi-automatic handguns can be fired either single-action or double-action. To open the action of a semi-automatic handgun, pull back the slide (top of the barrel) and lock it in place. To close the action, push the slide-release lever or button.

Semi-automatic handguns (left) and revolvers (right) are the two most common handgun actions.

To load a revolver, swing the cylinder out or load through a loading gate at the rear of the cylinder.

Semi-automatic handguns store cartridges in a magazine that slides into the grip.

Remember, if there is a cartridge in the magazine of a semi-automatic handgun, working the action will load a round into the firing chamber. Always keep your finger off the trigger when not firing.

Caution: If there is a cartridge in the gun's magazine when you open and close the action of a semi-automatic handgun, a cartridge will be loaded into the firing chamber and the gun will be ready to fire. Be careful during loading and unloading, and always have the muzzle of a handgun pointed in a safe direction while doing so.

Bolt-action handguns operate just like bolt-action rifles and shotguns. To open the action, raise the bolt and slide it back until it stops. To close the action, slide the bolt forward again and back down into its original position, locking the bolt in place.

Hinge-action (or break-action) handguns are not as common as revolvers or semi-automatic handguns. Hinge-action handguns are usually single-shot and fired single-action.

Handgun Sights

Because handguns are similar to rifles, they have similar sighting systems. Most have open or iron sights, but some handguns can also be fitted with scopes or laser sights. It is more difficult to accurately shoot handguns than rifles. First, there is less distance between the front and rear sight of a handgun than a rifle, making aiming more difficult. Second, holding a handgun in your hand(s) rather than against your shoulder also makes it more difficult to aim accurately. As a result, very few handguns are used for hunting when compared to rifles and shotguns. But handguns are still fun to shoot, and many competition shooters choose handguns for that reason.

Use the Safety!

Unlike most shoulder guns, handguns may not come equipped with a safety that disables the firing mechanism. If a handgun has a safety, use it. Never totally depend on a safety. Even with a gun safety in the "On" or "Safe" position, a gun could fire if dropped. If a handgun does not have a safety, use extra caution.

Modern muzzleloaders are no longer considered "primitive" weapons.

MUZZLELOADERS

Mention the word muzzleloader to most sportsmen and the image of a buckskin-clad frontiersman comes to mind. Early firearms were known as muzzleloaders because they were loaded from the muzzle, not the breech of the gun. Today, most modern firearms are loaded from the breech, that end of the barrel opposite the muzzle. Early rifles, shotguns, and handguns were all muzzleloaders.

As you might expect, it took practice to learn to quickly load and fire a muzzleloader. Soldiers during the Revolutionary War were expected to be able to load and fire their muzzleloader at least three times per minute. Some frontiersmen even learned to load and fire their muzzleloader while on the run, no doubt saving their lives at times. Early muzzleloaders either had rifled barrels or were smoothbores. Smoothbores were also known as muskets. Like rifles, muskets fired a single bullet, but were less accurate than rifles because of no rifling in the barrel.

Even though muzzleloaders were the earliest of firearms, they are still used for shooting and hunting today. Many shooters and hunters prefer doing things the "old-fashioned way," so they enjoy shooting muzzleloaders. Most states and provinces even have special muzzleloading hunting seasons, allowing hunters to extend the time they spend in the field each year. Check your local hunting regulations brochure.

Muzzleloaders are loaded from the muzzle of the gun by use of a ramrod.

Modern muzzleloaders are anything but primitive. Accurate and dependable, modern muzzleloading rifles can kill a deer or other big-game animal at ranges of several hundred yards. Though most muzzleloaders have open sights, some modern muzzleloaders have been fitted with telescopic sights for long-range shooting. Most modern muzzleloaders are percussion cap firearms, but some flintlock guns are still made. If you ever have the chance to shoot a muzzleloader, especially a flintlock, make sure that you wear eye protection, as the fire and smoke from such a gun will be much more than when shooting a breech-loading firearm.

A new kind of muzzleloader, developed in recent years, is the inline muzzleloader. With inlines, the percussion cap and its flash hole are moved from the side of the gun to the rear of the barrel, in other words "in-line" with the barrel. Doing so makes the gun easier to clean and more reliable than a standard muzzleloader.

You may notice that some muzzleloaders have two triggers, one in front of the other. If that is the case, one of the triggers, usually the front trigger, is known as a "set" trigger. By pulling the set trigger, a shooter sets the rear or main trigger so that touching it even lightly fires the gun. Again, once a set trigger on a muzzleloader has been pulled, just brushing the main trigger could fire the gun, so beware and be ready.

One last, very important thing to remember about muzzleloaders: They should always be loaded with black powder (or an approved black-powder substitute, such as Pyrodex), never with modern, smokeless gunpowder. Smokeless gunpowder, such as that loaded in modern rifle, handgun, and shotgun ammunition, is too powerful for muzzleloaders and may cause them to explode when fired. Read your gun's instruction manual before loading a muzzleloader or, if there is no instruction manual for your gun, check with a gunsmith about safe loading practices.

Three Main Parts of a Muzzleloader

Just as modern rifles and shotguns have three main parts—barrel, action, and stock—muzzleloaders have those same three parts. The only difference is that the action of a muzzleloader is called a "lock." In modern firearms, a gun's action loads, fires the gun, and ejects the empty cartridge or shot shell case. A muzzleloader, however, is loaded manually, and there is no empty cartridge or shot shell case to eject. In simplest terms, the lock of a muzzleloader is the firing mechanism of the gun. In a flintlock muzzleloader, the lock consists of a hammer, priming pan, and frizzen. In a percussion cap muzzleloader, the lock is made up of a hammer and nipple, the nipple being that small part of the lock the percussion cap fits over.

Modern inline muzzleloaders can be fitted with telescopic sights for accuracy.

Only black powder or Pyrodex should be fired in muzzleloaders, never modern, smokeless powder.

Loading a Muzzleloader

To load a muzzleloader, a measured amount of gunpowder is first poured down the barrel of the gun. A small piece of cloth, known as a patch, is then placed over the muzzle. A round lead ball or cone-shaped lead bullet is placed over the patch. Both the patch and ball or patch and bullet are then pushed down the barrel and seated against the gunpowder by using a long wood, fiberglass, or metal rod, called a ramrod.

In muzzleloading shotguns, an added step is required when loading. Because loose shot is loaded in a shotgun instead of a single bullet, a covering known as a card is needed over the shot to keep it from rolling out the end of the barrel before the gun is fired. This card is tamped down over the shot with the ramrod as the final step in loading a muzzleloading shotgun.

Original muzzleloading rifles, shotguns, and handguns all had priming pans located near the rear of the barrel. A small amount of gunpowder was placed in the priming pan. When the gunpowder in the priming pan was ignited, the fire from the burning powder flashed through a small hole at the rear of the barrel—known as the flash hole—and set off the main powder charge, firing the gun. How the powder in the priming pan in early muzzleloaders was ignited is what gave the guns their names.

Muzzleloader Safety

Muzzleloaders, even new models, are less dependable than other firearms. For instance, muzzleloaders can "hang fire," meaning that even though you pull the trigger and the gunpowder in the priming pan is ignited or the percussion cap fires, the main powder charge inside the barrel does not immediately ignite. Instead, the gunpowder smolders for a time before it catches and finally ignites, firing the gun. Obviously, this situation can be very dangerous, and a muzzleloader shooter must know how to handle such a situation.

If you do experience a hang fire, the first thing to do is keep the muzzle of the gun pointed downrange. It could be several seconds, several minutes, or even longer before a muzzleloader finally decides to fire. If it doesn't, first try repriming the gun and firing it again. If the gun refuses to fire after several attempts at repriming, you are faced with the problem of how to extract the bullet and patch from the barrel, dump out the powder, and reload.

The danger in this procedure is having the gun go off while attempting to extract the bullet. To prevent this, wise shooters pour water into the flash hole as well as down the barrel to extinguish any spark that might be lingering in the main powder charge. Once you are certain the gun won't fire, attaching a corkscrew device (known as a ball puller) to the end of the ramrod will allow you to tap into the lead bullet and pull it from the barrel. A safer, more modern solution for removing a load from a muzzleloader is to attach a specialized CO_2 cartridge to the flash hole of a gun and blow the bullet, powder, and patch out.

The best way to handle a hang fire is to avoid one in the first place. Keeping your black powder or Pyrodex totally dry is the key, as well as tamping it tightly into place in the bottom of the gun barrel with the ramrod before loading the patch and bullet.

Another technique muzzle-loader shooters use to make their shooting as safe as possible is marking their ramrod with two lines to prevent double loading.

Modern inline muzzleloaders have their flash hole "in line" with the rear of the barrel.

The first line marks the depth of an empty barrel and the second line marks the depth of a loaded barrel. This prevents the shooter from forgetting he has already loaded his gun and mistakenly loading it a second time. It may sound unbelievable, but double loading happens more often than you might think. By having your ramrod marked with two lines, you can quickly know whether your muzzleloader is loaded or unloaded.

One final tip: When hunting with a muzzleloader for two or more days in succession, it is always best to fire the gun at the end of each day rather than

PARTS OF SPEECH FROM THE KENTUCKY RIFLE

Flintlock muzzleloading rifles of 200 years ago not only helped America's frontiersmen hunt game and protect themselves, but also gave us several sayings that remain in our language yet today. For instance:

Muzzleloaders have been around so long that parts of speech from the gun have become sayings in the English language.

· "Lock, stock, and barrel" refers to the three main parts of every rifle—in other words, the whole thing.

· "Going off half-cocked" means a gun firing from the halfcock position, before it is expected to.

· "Flash in the pan" describes a flash of gunpowder in the priming pan that didn't ignite the main powder charge.

So before you decide to jump into something lock, stock, and barrel, remember not to go off half-cocked, or you may end up just a flash in the pan!

MUZZLELOADER HISTORY

The matchlock was an early firearm that actually had a wick like a candle that a shooter had to light. When the trigger of a matchlock gun was pulled, the wick lowered into the gunpowder in the priming pan, firing the gun. It's easy to imagine that anyone trying to shoot or hunt with a matchlock firearm would have had a tough time getting the gun to fire consistently on windy or rainy days. Matchlock firearms were used in Europe until about 1700, and by the first Europeans arriving in America.

The wheel lock was a step advanced from the matchlock because it was the first firearm to use flint and steel to produce a spark. It also was the first firearm to have a covered priming pan, making shooting or hunting in windy or rainy weather less of a problem. In a wheel lock, a small, spring-loaded wheel near the rear of the barrel was wound tight with a key. When the trigger of the gun was pulled, the steel wheel spun against a piece of flint, causing sparks. The sparks set off the gunpowder in the priming pan, which in turn set off the main powder charge.

A flintlock gun was the gun that many frontiersmen and pioneers carried when North America was first being settled by Europeans. Popular from the 1600s well into the 1800s, flintlocks were sometimes called long rifles because of their long, thin barrels. Flintlocks were made all over the Eastern U. S. by early gunsmiths, but some of the best came from Pennsylvania and Kentucky, earning the gun its generic name—Kentucky long rifle.

In a flintlock, the hammer holds a piece of flint that strikes a steel plate (called a frizzen) when the trigger is pulled, causing sparks. These sparks set off the gunpowder in the priming pan, which sets off the main powder charge. Have you ever heard the expression, "Keep your powder dry?" The saying comes from keeping the powder dry in a flintlock gun's priming pan so the gun will fire.

The flintlock was eventually replaced by the percussion cap gun. The percussion cap itself was a small, metal cap that fit over the flash hole of a muzzleloader. When the hammer of a gun hit the percussion cap, the cap exploded, sending a small amount of fire through the flash hole, igniting the main powder charge.

The advantage of a percussion cap was that loose gunpowder, exposed to the weather, was no longer needed in a priming pan on the outside of a gun. As a result, percussion cap guns were more reliable than flintlocks. The invention of the percussion cap eventually led to the development of today's self-contained rifle cartridges, handgun cartridges, and shotgun shells. Percussion caps are essentially the primers found in today's modern center-fire ammunition.

just remove the priming powder or percussion cap and leaving the charge in the barrel. Leaving a charge in the barrel overnight can cause the gunpowder to draw moisture, preventing the gun from firing the next day. Completely reload the gun each morning, and you are assured it will fire when expected— or at least as certain as things get in muzzleloading.

When compared with more modern firearms, muzzleloaders require a lot of added equipment. All that equipment is held in a bag known as a "possibles" sack.

HANDLING & MAINTAINING FIREARMS

Shooting and hunting are among the safest of all outdoor sports. According to the latest statistics from the National Shooting Sports Foundation (NSSF), baseball, basketball, football, and soccer all have higher injury rates than shooting and hunting. But if an accident does happen while shooting or hunting, it will likely be serious. If you remember to apply the following three

Statistically, shooting and hunting are among the safest of all outdoor sports.

primary safe gun-handling practices, your chances of ever being involved in a shooting or hunting accident will be greatly reduced.

The first rule is to treat every gun as if it is loaded at all times, and it means just that—all times. For instance, when taking a gun from a gun safe, transport case, or rack, or if someone hands you a firearm, always assume that the gun is loaded. The first thing you should do is point the muzzle in a safe direction, then open the action and check to make sure that the gun is unloaded.

It doesn't matter if you're positive the gun is unloaded. It doesn't matter if you saw the person who handed you the gun open the action and check it. The first thing you do is open the action yourself and check to make sure that it is unloaded, every time. Get into that positive habit as a young shooter, and you will continue to do it throughout your life. It's amazing how many people have been shot or killed by guns they thought or were told were unloaded.

The second rule is to always keep the muzzle of a gun pointed in a safe direction. This is easy to remember if you think about a dog. The muzzle of a dog is that part of the animal that can bite you. It's the same with a gun. The muzzle of a firearm is the end of the barrel, the part that can "bite" you. The muzzle can also "bite" someone else if the gun should happen to go off unexpectedly.

But even if a gun does fire unexpectedly, it will not harm you or anyone else if the muzzle is pointed in a safe direction. Most of the time that safe direction will be up, but depending upon the shooting/hunting situation, the safest direction to point a muzzle may be down, to the side, front, or back. In their simplest form, guns are just pieces of metal, wood, and plastic. They have no brains; they cannot think. Therefore, you have to do their thinking for them. Safe gun handling is not rocket science, but you do have to apply what you've learned, every time.

The third rule is never to point a gun at anything you do not intend to shoot. This applies whether a gun is loaded or unloaded. A practical example of this would be when using a firearm with a telescopic sight for hunting. Never use the scope as a pair of binoculars, as you have to point the gun to do so. In other words, never look through the scope when scouting for game. A scope should only be used when actually aiming and firing a shotgun, rifle, or handgun. NEVER point a firearm at someone as a joke, even with the safety on or the gun unloaded.

Using the shoulder carry allows your free hand and arm to rest.

The sling carry allows both of your hands to be free. A sling can also be used for steadying a rifle when aiming and firing.

This young hunter is using a cradle carry.

Gun Carrying Positions

There are six common gun carrying positions: double-handed, cradle, elbow, shoulder, trail, and sling. The six positions can be safely used for carrying a gun either when shooting or hunting. But when using any of these positions you must keep in mind where other shooters in your party are located and adjust your carry accordingly, so that the muzzle of your gun is always pointed in a safe direction.

One advantage of the sling carry is that it leaves both of your hands free.

· The double-handed carry gives you the most control of a firearm because both of your hands are on the gun at the same time. Your trigger hand should be placed around the small of the stock—also known as the pistol grip—while your other hand grips the forearm of the gun. In this position, the muzzle of the gun is usually pointed up slightly, either to the right or left.

· In the cradle carry, your trigger hand is again around the pistol grip, with the forearm of the gun resting in the crook of your other arm, like cradling a baby. In this position, the muzzle of the gun is pointed to the side.

· With the elbow carry, the gun rests in the bend of your arm with your other hand free. This is a good way to rest your free arm and hand while hunting or shooting. In this carry, the gun muzzle is pointed toward the ground.

· When using the shoulder carry, one hand is around the pistol grip of the gun and the top of the barrel rests on your shoulder, leaving your other hand free. Shotgun shooters often use this grip, as there is no rear sight on most shotguns to dig into your shoulder. In this grip, the muzzle is pointed behind you and up.

· The trail carry is also a one-handed carry. The gun is grasped somewhere in the middle, near its balancing point. With a trail carry, the muzzle of the gun is usually pointed forward, so never use this carry if someone is walking in front of you.

· A sling carry is used by shooters who have a sling on their firearm, and is a simple matter of placing the sling over one of your shoulders; the gun

Adequate eye and hearing protection should be an important part of your basic shooting equipment.

then hangs down your back. If you are walking a long distance, a gun sling can be pulled over one shoulder and your head—worn bandolier style—to prevent the sling from sliding off your shoulder in rough terrain.

An advantage of adding a sling to your gun is that it leaves both of your hands free when using this carry. Most big-game hunters have slings on their rifles and some shotgun shooters, such as turkey, deer, and waterfowl hunters, do as well. In addition to making guns easier to carry, some slings can also be adjusted to help steady a rifle while aiming and firing. In a sling carry, the muzzle of the gun is pointed up.

Cleaning Firearms

When you return home or to your camp from shooting or hunting, firearms should be cleaned before putting them away—every time. This is especially true if the gun has become wet, such as when shooting or hunting in rain or snow. Duck or goose hunting near water can be especially hard on firearms, so special care should be given to guns when hunting in these areas.

Putting a wet, dirty gun in a gun safe or gun case and forgetting it until the next time you want to shoot or hunt is a poor practice. A dirty gun will not

Immediately clean your firearm each time after returning from shooting or hunting, and it will last a lifetime and hold its value.

work as well as a clean firearm—it may even become dangerous to hunt with over time—and should rust or other corrosion develop, the gun will eventually lose its value. Firearms are not inexpensive, but will hold their value and last a lifetime if you take proper care of them. Here's how...

Before cleaning any firearm, first make sure that the gun is unloaded! Firearms should never be brought into a house or other building loaded in the first place, but you should always check to make sure that a gun is unloaded before beginning cleaning. Any ammunition should also be put away, not left on the cleaning table.

Begin by breaking down the firearm into as many pieces as conveniently possible. With a hinge-action gun, for example, remove the forearm, then separate the stock from the barrel. With a pump or semi-automatic firearm, slide or lock the bolt back and remove the barrel. With a bolt-action gun, remove the bolt. With a lever action, open the action by moving the lever all the way down until it stops. If you don't know how to break down your gun for cleaning, refer to the owner's manual. If your gun doesn't have an owner's manual, take it to a gunsmith and he can show you how to break down the gun for cleaning.

Black-powder residue can be very corrosive, so muzzleloaders need to be thoroughly cleaned at the end of each shooting day.

Once the gun is apart or the action is open, swab the barrel with powder solvent. This liquid loosens the gunpowder residue in the barrel, making it easier to remove. You do this by putting a small amount of solvent on a piece of cloth, known as a patch, and working the patch back and forth through the barrel several times on the end of a cleaning rod. Next, screw a metal bore brush onto the tip of the cleaning rod and work it through the barrel several times. This brushing helps loosen powder residue. Replace the brush with a dry patch and continue running patches through the barrel until one finally comes out clean. Lastly, put a small amount of gun oil on a clean patch and run it through the barrel. The inside of the gun barrel is now clean.

To clean the outside of a gun barrel, lightly spray it with gun oil and wipe off the excess oil with a soft cloth. Do the same with the other parts of the gun, stock included, and reassemble your firearm. If you don't use your firearms for long periods of time, such as during the spring or summer, it's good to take them out every few months and wipe them down with an oily rag to prevent rust. Running an oily patch through the barrel is also a good idea. Once per year, guns should be broken down and cleaned even more thoroughly than just described. If you don't know how to do this, a gunsmith can tell you how or do it for you.

Storing Firearms

How and where you store firearms at home is important for keeping family members and others who might visit your home safe. If possible, guns should be stored in a locked gun safe and all ammunition should be stored in a separate, locked location. That way if an inexperienced person, such as your younger brother or sister, should somehow happen to get their hands on your gun, they won't have the ammunition too.

If you don't own a lockable gun safe, individual gun locks can be purchased inexpensively that will fit on a gun, preventing it from firing. Some firearms now come with locking devices already built into them. But whether stored in a locked gun safe or elsewhere, firearms should always be stored unloaded. They should also be transported unloaded and in a gun transport case of some type. Soft-sided gun cases are good for most hunting trips close to home. When traveling long distances to hunt, such as by airplane, hard-sided gun cases protect firearms better. Make sure that you check local regulations before transporting a firearm and ammunition in a vehicle or by air so that you know how to do so legally.

In a vehicle, guns should be transported to the hunting field or shooting range in a gun case.

Another thing to consider these days concerning home gun storage is break-ins. It seems that burglaries are happening more and more often, and if a burglar should break into your house, will he be able to find your gun(s) easily and steal them? Give this some serious thought. Only you know where it's best to hide your guns in your house if you don't have a lockable gun safe.

A final consideration is keeping a loaded gun in the house for self-protection. Some people insist on keeping a loaded handgun in the drawer of their bedside stand, but this is seldom a good idea. Family members and friends—not just criminals—are sometimes accidentally shot and killed by these loaded handguns. In most cases, a gun should not be loaded while in the house.

Transporting Firearms

Unless you're lucky enough to live in a rural area where you can go shooting or hunting right from your home, you will likely have to transport your firearms to a shooting range or hunting area by vehicle. To do so, you must transport guns both safely and legally.

The most important thing to remember when transporting firearms is that they must be unloaded while in a vehicle. Second, they should be transported in a gun case, rack, box, or other container made for a firearm. But these are just general gun transportation rules. Make sure to check your individual state or provincial laws before transporting a firearm in a vehicle, as more specific, stringent transport rules or laws may apply for your area.

When transporting a firearm in the field, such as in a boat, on an ATV, or snowmobile, the same safety rules apply. Always have the gun unloaded and secured in a case or rack. When waterfowl hunting, it's a good idea to transport your gun in a floating gun case while in a boat so that you don't lose your firearm should it somehow go overboard.

A hard-sided, lockable gun case is necessary for traveling on commercial airlines with a firearm.

A Few Safety Tips

In addition to the three main gun safety rules, there are a few more things to keep in mind when handling firearms. Some of the following tips apply to shooting, some to hunting, but most apply to both:

Make Sure the Barrel is Clear of Obstructions

Even a small amount of mud or snow in the end of a gun barrel may cause the barrel to explode when the gun is fired. If you happen to slip and fall while shooting or hunting, and at some time you will, take the time to unload your firearm and check to make sure that nothing is lodged in the barrel. If you do find an obstruction, remove it. In the field, you may have to cut a thin stick to push down the barrel. If that doesn't work, possibly a gun cleaning rod will do the trick once you get home or back to your vehicle. If you can't remove the obstruction, take your gun to a gunsmith to have him remove the object and make the gun safe to fire. Again, your gun should be unloaded while attempting to remove an obstruction, including all cartridges or shells held in the magazine.

Only Carry Ammunition for the Gun You are Shooting

Just because a rifle cartridge, handgun cartridge, or shotgun shell will fit into the firing chamber of a gun does not mean that it is safe to shoot in that gun. You must match the specific ammunition with the specific caliber or gauge of gun you will be shooting. During the fun and excitement of shooting or hunting, it is possible to get ammunition mixed up if you carry different sizes of ammo with you. For example, a 20-gauge shotgun shell can mistakenly be loaded into a 12-gauge shotgun barrel. The smaller 20-gauge shell will slide about a third of the way down the barrel of the larger gauge gun and become stuck. A 12-gauge shell can then be loaded behind the 20-gauge shell into the firing chamber, as normal. What do you suppose will happen to that gun when the trigger is pulled? What do you suppose will happen to the shooter or hunter holding that firearm? If the barrel explodes, as it will, the result will not be pretty. A serious injury will occur. Remember, only carry ammunition for the gun you are currently hunting with or shooting.

Be Sure of Your Target & Beyond

When shooting or hunting, it is the shooter's/hunter's responsibility to make sure of the target and what's beyond that target. Do you know for sure what you're shooting at? Is that a deer in the brush or another hunter wearing a brown coat? Is that a squirrel at the base of a tree, or another hunter sitting there moving his hand? It might sound silly, but every year hunters are shot by other hunters who mistake them for game animals. Take a second and even a third look to make absolutely sure that what you are shooting at is what you think it is.

And hit or miss, do you know where your bullet or shot pellets will stop? Sometimes a bullet from a rifle or handgun can pass completely through a game animal and come out the other side intact with enough energy to keep going a long distance. Do you know where that bullet will finally land? You should, because you're responsible for it. A bullet from a high-powered rifle can travel several miles. Even a small-caliber rifle bullet, such as a .22, has a range of over a mile (over 1.6 km). And shot pellets from a shotgun can travel hundreds of yards. Make sure of your target and beyond. Shooting into the base of a hill or at a down angle, as when hunting from a treestand, will assure that your bullet stops where you want it to.

Always be aware of not only what is in front of your target, but beyond, as well.

When crossing an obstacle, such as a fence, while hunting, all guns should first be unloaded. You also must have permission from the landowner to hunt on private property.

Don't Cross a Fence, Stream, or Ditch with a Loaded Gun

In the field, hunters must continually cross obstacles—it's just part of hunting. But when you come to a fence, stream, ditch, or other obstacle, resist the temptation to get across as quickly as possible. Take the time to first unload your gun, then cross. After all, you won't be able to shoot accurately if a game animal should appear while you're crossing the obstacle, so why take a chance of injuring yourself or someone else with a loaded gun? Unload first, then cross.

When hunting with another hunter, the safest way to cross an obstacle, say a fence, is for both hunters to unload, then one person takes both guns while the other hunter crosses. Once the first hunter is over the fence, the guns are handed over the fence and the second hunter crosses. Only then do the hunters reload and resume hunting.

And keep in mind, too, that no landowner wants his fence damaged by a hunter who crosses improperly. If possible, roll under a fence or climb over at a fence post. Mashing down a fence between posts or causing other damage such as fence staples to pull out will lose you a hunting spot on private property quicker than anything. Remember to treat private hunting land as you would your own, and you'll be welcomed back by the landowner.

Never Shoot at a Flat or Hard Surface

A ricochet is the term used for a bullet or shotgun pellets bouncing off a hard surface, such as a rock or even water. The problem with a ricochet is that you never know in which direction the bullet or shot will go. It may veer off at a sharp angle or may fly back at you, the shooter. Even the flat surface of a lake or pond can cause a bullet or shot to ricochet if you shoot at a low enough angle.

I remember waterfowl hunting once when another hunter, in a hunting blind several hundred yards away, shot a duck from the sky that fell onto the water crippled. The hunter had to shoot the crippled duck a second time, on the water, a standard practice in waterfowl hunting. But when the hunter fired the second time, a single pellet from that shot bounced off the water, flew across the marsh, and struck me in the chest. Thankfully, the shotgun pellet was traveling slowly by the time it got to me so that it did not even penetrate my hunting coat, but the incident shows how uncontrollable a ricochet can be. And what injury might have happened if the pellet had struck one of my eyes? It should be noted that the hunter was not shooting directly in my direction, but off to the side. Again, you never know which way a ricochet will go.

STORING YOUR FIREARM: GUN SAFE OR GUN LOCK?

Guns at home should always be stored unloaded, ideally in a lockable gun safe or lockable gun cabinet. This keeps guns out of the reach of children or careless adults. It also prevents your guns from being stolen should a thief break into your house.

But gun safes or gun cabinets can be expensive for a young shooter. An alternative is to buy a gun lock for each of your firearms. Gun locks are inexpensive and block the trigger or gun action so that the gun cannot be fired. Always lock your firearms when not using them, and only you and your parents should know where the keys to your gun locks are kept. Never show the hiding place of your keys to a younger brother, sister, or friends who are not mature enough to handle firearms safely. Ammunition should be stored separately from firearms and in a locked ammunition box.

Archery can be just as much fun as shooting firearms, as long as it is done safely. Remember, a bow and arrows are not toys.

chapter 2

ARCHERY

Humans have been shooting and hunting with bows and arrows for thousands of years. Ancient cave paintings show hunters using bows and arrows. There are some primitive cultures in the world yet today who hunt exclusively with bows and arrows.

Just as firearms have three primary safety rules, so do bows and arrows. Know and apply them, and your chances of ever being involved in a bow shooting or bowhunting accident will be greatly reduced:

1. Always point an arrow in a safe direction.
2. Never draw an arrow until you are ready to shoot.
3. Never point a bow and arrow at anything you do not intend to shoot.

HOW BOWS ARE NAMED

There are four types of bows: longbows, recurve bows, compound bows, and crossbows.

Longbows are the oldest of the four bow designs. The earliest longbows were a slim, strong, flexible piece of wood. A section of animal leg tendon was tied to each end of the longbow as a bowstring. Because of the longbow's design, it takes a lot of strength to pull back an arrow and hold it at full draw. As a result, very few archers today shoot or hunt with a true longbow.

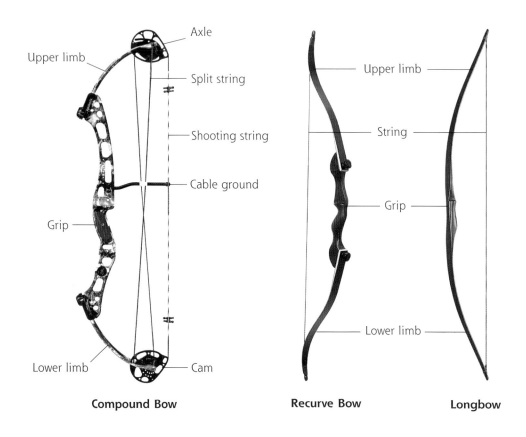

Upper limb

Axle

Split string

Shooting string

Cable ground

Grip

Lower limb

Cam

Compound Bow

Upper limb

String

Grip

Lower limb

Recurve Bow

Longbow

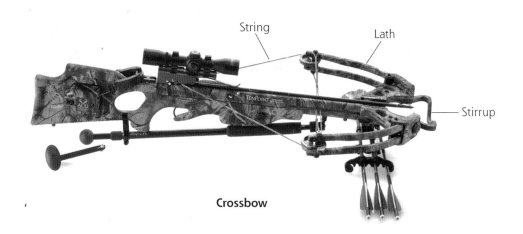

String

Lath

Stirrup

Crossbow

At times in the past, however, before the invention of firearms, longbows were used not only for hunting, but also as weapons of war. Armies used bows and arrows as long-range weapons on the battlefield.

Recurve Bows were an advance over longbows. The ends of a recurve bow are bent away from the shooter (recurved), giving the bow more power but with less overall length than a longbow. Some bowhunters hunt with recurve bows yet today.

Compound Bows were developed during the second half of the 20th century, and use a system of cams or pulleys and cables to make the bowstring easier to pull and hold at full draw. This is accomplished by a feature known as "let-off." The advantage of let-off is that a shooter is not holding the full draw weight of the bow when at full draw. For example, with an 80-pound (36.4 kg) compound bow, the shooter might be holding only 40 pounds (18.2 kg) at full draw, possibly even less. As a result, most archers and hunters can shoot compound bows more accurately than longbows and recurve bows. Also, compound bows are usually not as long as longbows and recurves, making them more popular with bowhunters, especially when shooting from a tight space such as a treestand.

Crossbows were developed during the Middle Ages as weapons of war. Today, they are used for hunting, especially big game such as deer. Some states and provinces even have special crossbow hunting seasons, which can extend a hunter's time in the woods each year. A crossbow is simply a short longbow or recurve bow that has been laid on its side and mounted on a gun stock. Like a rifle or shotgun, a shooter grips a crossbow by the stock and holds it against the shoulder for firing. The string of a crossbow is pulled back either by hand or by using a cocking device. The string locks in place at full draw and is released by pulling a trigger, similar to firing a gun. Some crossbows have safety latches that prevent them from firing unexpectedly, but others do not, so be careful. Always know the safety features of the particular crossbow you are shooting.

PARTS OF A BOW

In its most basic form—longbows and recurve bows—a bow is simply a curved piece of wood or composite material with a bowstring attached. An archer holds the bow in the middle by the grip. The part of the bow above the grip is called the upper limb and the part below the grip is the lower limb. The notched end of the arrow attaches to the bowstring at the nock point, and the arrow shaft lies on the arrow rest. Compound bows and compound crossbows have additional parts, such as cam wheels, pulleys, cables, and possibly a cable guard, which prevents the bowstring from hitting the cables. Crossbows also have a stock. An accessory that some bowhunters attach to their bowstring is a string silencer, which helps muffle the twanging sound a bow can make when an arrow is released.

Some bows, such as recurve bows, should be unstrung when not in use. The safest way to do this is with a bowstringer. A bowstringer is a piece of stout cord with a leather cup on each end. One cup is placed over each end of the bow. To string a recurve bow safely, place the belly of the cord of the bowstringer on the floor and step on it with your foot. By pulling up on the bow, you can then slide the two ends of the bowstring into place. To unstring a recurve bow, reverse the procedure. Using a bowstringer is the best and safest way to string and unstring a recurve bow because it does not twist the bow limbs. Compound bows and crossbows do not need to be unstrung when not in use.

Safety note: Never pull a bowstring back and release it without an arrow on the string. This is called dry-firing a bow. Not only is dry-firing hard on bow limbs, it could also result in injury to the shooter.

Draw Weight & Draw Length

The draw weight of a bow refers to the amount of force required to pull a bowstring back to full draw, usually a distance of 28 inches (71.1 cm). For example, if a bow has a draw weight of 50 pounds (22.7 kg) that means it takes 50 pounds (22.7 kg) of force to pull the bowstring back on that particular bow and hold it at full draw.

If you're new to shooting a bow, it's better to begin with a bow that's easier for you to pull rather than harder. By shooting a bow with a lighter draw weight, you'll be able to learn the basics of bow shooting and develop good shooting habits without the struggle of trying to pull back and hold a bow that's too powerful for you. As you progress in your shooting and your back and arm muscles develop, you can then graduate to a bow with a higher draw weight.

Draw length has to do with the actual measurement—in inches (centimeters)—of how far an arrow is drawn when pulled to full draw. Because different people have different arm lengths, not everyone will have the same arrow draw length. When buying a bow and matching set of arrows, it is helpful to have a knowledgeable

When first learning to shoot a bow and arrow, it is better to have a bow that is easier to pull and hold at full draw rather than one that's more difficult to pull.

person accurately measure your draw length. You can then have arrows cut especially for you and your specific draw length. A good rule of thumb for beginning shooters is to have arrows that are a little long rather than arrows that are too short. That way, if you accidentally overdraw the bow (pull it back too far) the arrow still stays on the arrow rest; it doesn't come off and possibly injure your hand or arm.

PARTS OF AN ARROW

Arrows are the thin projectiles shot from longbows, recurve bows, compound bows, and crossbows, but not all arrows are alike. Arrows have a certain stiffness to their shaft, called spine, and that stiffness must be matched to the particular bow you are shooting. If arrows aren't matched to a bow, a serious injury could occur to the shooter. For instance, if an arrow has too much bend, in other words is not stiff enough for a particular bow, it might shatter when released from the bowstring. Arrows shot from a crossbow are usually shorter than arrows shot from longbows, recurve bows, and compound bows. There are five main parts to most arrows: nock, fletching, shaft, crest, and tip.

The nock is the rear, notched rear end of the arrow that fits on the bowstring. On modern arrows, the nock is usually made of a colored piece of plastic.

Fletching is the group of feathers or plastic vanes glued on the shaft near the rear of an arrow. Years ago, Native Americans made arrows with fletching of split turkey-wing feathers. Today, most fletching is made from a variety of synthetic materials. Fletching stabilizes an arrow in flight, helping it fly straighter and as a result be more accurate.

In addition, fletching is usually in groups of three or four feathers or vanes. If in a grouping of three, one of the three feathers will be a different color than the other two. This odd-colored feather is called the cock feather. For an arrow to shoot as accurately as possible, the cock feather must be at a 90-degree angle from the bow when the arrow is placed on the bowstring.

The shaft of an arrow is the main body. Originally made from wood, arrow shafts today are made from many materials in addition to wood: aluminum, fiberglass, carbon fiber, and others. The shaft of an arrow is what sits on the bow's arrow rest when the arrow is nocked and the string is pulled.

The crest of an arrow is the colored band painted around the shaft. The crest helps archers tell arrows apart if more than one person is shooting at the same target. Most hunting arrows today do not have colored crests, as usually the entire arrow is painted in a camouflage pattern, fletching included.

The tip of an arrow is the point. There are several different tips that archers and hunters can put on their arrows. Target tips are used for shooting at standard round archery targets, straw bales, or full-body, foam animal targets. Field points are used for shooting stumps and other natural objects when an archer is roaming through the woods, practice shooting. Blunt tips are used for hunting small-game animals, such as rabbits or squirrels. Broadheads are used for hunting big game, such as deer, elk, and moose. Some broadheads have fixed blades, while others have moveable blades. Broadhead blades are razor sharp and should be handled with extreme care. Even lightly touching a broadhead with your finger or other part of your body can cause a serious cut. The safest way to install and remove a broadhead from an arrow is with a broadhead wrench made especially for that purpose.

Be sure that you closely inspect each arrow after every shot. Arrows can and will crack occasionally, even through normal use. If you shoot a cracked arrow by mistake, it could snap in half when coming off the bowstring and cause injury, either to you or to someone standing nearby. Should you notice that one of your arrows is cracked, bent, or warped in any way, carefully break it or cut it in half and discard it. That way, no one will be tempted to shoot the broken arrow.

SHOOTING A BOW

The shooting methods of firearms and those of bows and arrows have some similarities. For example, like handguns and shotguns, most bows are shot from a standing position. And like a rifle shooter, an archer stands at a 90-degree angle to the target.

The main difference between shooting a bow and arrows and shooting firearms is that a bow must be brought to full draw to shoot an arrow. This means that an archer grasps the bowstring, or a handheld mechanical release that grips the bowstring, and pulls back. If grasping the bowstring itself, most archers

Start close to the target when learning the basics of archery. The hits will help build your confidence.

use a three-finger grip. The index finger is usually placed above the arrow on the bowstring, with the second and third fingers of the hand placed below the arrow. However, some archers prefer three fingers below the arrow. Try the two different three-finger styles, as well as a mechanical bowstring release, and see what feels more comfortable for you and how your arrows are most accurate.

To be most accurate, an archer pulls the bowstring back the same distance and to the same spot on his face each time. This spot is called an anchor point, and is different for different archers. Some archers anchor to the corner of their mouth, some to the side of their nose, and some under their chin. A small button on the bowstring, known as a "kisser," can be set up to touch the archer's lips when the bow is at full draw, anchored, and the arrow is ready to release. It doesn't matter where on your face you anchor, the important thing is that the bowstring, arrow nock, or kisser button comes to the same anchor point each time you draw.

Good archers also know that a smooth release of the bowstring must be followed by a good follow-through. This means holding the bow in place with your bow hand until the arrow hits the target. If you get in the bad habit of dropping your bow hand or arm after an arrow is released, you will not be as accurate as when you consistently follow through.

ARCHERY ACCESSORIES

Various pieces of archery equipment make shooting or hunting with bows and arrows easier and more fun.

Guards, Gloves & Releases

An armguard protects the bowstring from slapping your wrist or the forearm of your bow arm when releasing an arrow, which can be painful. When bowhunting in cold weather, an armguard also helps keep heavy hunting clothes out of the path of the bowstring. If the bowstring catches clothing, it could send the arrow off course.

For grasping, pulling the bowstring, and releasing an arrow, most archers prefer wearing a shooting glove. This leather glove allows the bowstring to roll off your fingertips for a smooth arrow release, while at the same time protecting your fingers. Other archers prefer using a mechanical bowstring release.

Left: An armguard protects the inside of your forearm from getting slapped by the bowstring. Center: A three-fingered archery shooting glove helps protect the fingertips of your shooting hand. Right: Most archers use a three-finger grip to grasp the bowstring; their index finger is above the arrow nock and their middle and ring fingers are below.

Mechanical Bowstring Releases

Many archers today prefer to use a mechanical bowstring release rather than their fingers. A mechanical release attaches to the shooter's hand by means of a strap, and a small set of metal jaws on the release fits around the bowstring (or sometimes a small loop attached to the bowstring). An archer draws the bow by pulling back his bowstring hand and arm, then releases the arrow by touching the mechanical release's trigger, much the same as pulling the trigger on a firearm. Most bowhunters prefer this type of bowstring. A second type of mechanical bowstring releases an arrow not by pulling a trigger, but by the shooter simply tensing or flexing his back muscles. Many target shooters use this second type of bowstring release, believing that it makes their shooting more accurate.

Bow Sights

Before we get into the specifics of sighting systems, you should know that the instinctive method of shooting requires no sights at all. It's a simple method of constant practice, of trial and error. The archer shoots arrow after arrow until body and mind know instinctively how an arrow will fly at certain distances and where it will strike a target. To be a good instinctive archer, a lot of practice is required.

Pin sights are common additions to a bow's riser or grip. Several pins are usually used, one for sighting at each of various distances. You must know the distance to the target. If the target is 20 yards (18.3 m) away, for example, the shooter lines up his 20-yard (18.3 m) pin with the target, draws and releases an arrow. Some pin sights can even be lit for shooting or hunting in low-light conditions.

Accurately judging distance is the most important aspect of being able to consistently hit a target using pin sights. In hunting situations, some bowhunters use electronic range finders to help them accurately measure the distance from their treestand to various objects in the field. For example, if a game animal walks near an object, say a certain tree, the animal is close to the distance already measured. You can do the same thing with a steel measuring tape; it just takes a little more time and effort.

Another bow sight is a peep sight. In this sighting system, a small, round disk with a tiny hole in the center is placed in the bowstring. When the string is pulled back to full draw, the archer looks through the peep sight with one eye. The arrow tip is then used as the front sight. Once the arrow tip is lined up with the target, the arrow is released.

Most crossbows use open or iron sights, similar to those found on a rifle or handgun, but crossbows can also be fitted with telescopic sights.

Quivers

Quivers hold arrows, keeping them safe and out of the way until ready to shoot. Quivers can be mounted on a bow or worn on your belt, over your shoulder, or on your back. The main thing to remember when choosing a quiver is to select one that covers the arrow tips. A good quiver not only protects arrows

ARCHERY IN THE SCHOOLS

If you're interested in learning how to shoot a bow and arrow, you may have to look no further than your own school. The National Archery in the Schools Program (NASP) is nationwide, and promotes student education, physical education, and participation in the lifelong sport of archery. The program teaches International Style Target Archery in physical education classes, grades 4 through 12. Contact your physical education teacher to see if an NASP program is offered at your school. If it's not, teachers can get information about starting such a program by going online to http://www.nasparchery.com.

The National Archery in the Schools Program (NASP) is a joint venture between state Departments of Education and Natural Resources. Several archery equipment manufacturers and organizations are also partners (listed in the Appendix).

Quivers safely store and transport arrows until they are ready to be shot.

Quivers can be hung from your belt or over your shoulder, as well as be attached to a bow.

from damage during transport, but also protects you from the arrows. This is extremely important when carrying broadheads for hunting.

STORING & TRANSPORTING ARCHERY EQUIPMENT

The proper home storage of archery equipment keeps your gear in good working order and prevents it from getting into the wrong hands, such as a younger brother or sister. Bow storage cases—that can also double as transport cases—are available in both soft- and hard-sided models. Buying one that locks is worth the extra expense. Place your bow in the case and then store it in a dry location. In other words, setting or hanging your bow in the corner of a damp basement or an area of high humidity is not a good idea. And, if possible, choose an area of the house with a relatively stable temperature. An area with extreme temperature swings from hot to cold, such as in an attic, could possibly cause the bow limbs to warp.

Don't forget that proper arrow storage is just as important as proper bow storage. You don't want anyone unfamiliar with arrows to inadvertently come across them, especially an arrow carrying a broadhead. Arrows can be safely stored at home in the same quiver used for carrying them in the field. Also, try to store arrows vertically (standing up) instead of horizontally. The effects of gravity, over time, could cause an arrow shaft to bow slightly if stored horizontally, making the arrow shoot less accurately.

Once you've lined up a gun's sights with the target, take your time and squeeze the trigger of a rifle or handgun, never jerk it.

chapter 3

MARKSMANSHIP & SHOOTING FUNDAMENTALS

Once you've learned the basics of how firearms work and how to handle them safely, you'll want to become the best shot you possibly can. Becoming a good shot with a firearm or bow takes practice, but it's practice that's fun! Just don't be discouraged if you're not a crack shot the first time out. As you grow, learn, and continue to shoot, you'll see your shooting skills get better and better.

GET READY TO SHOOT

Do you remember the three main rules of safe gun handling? Without reading any further, try to list the three in your mind or on a piece of paper. If you're having trouble, here they are once again:

· Treat every gun as if it is loaded at all times.

· Always keep the muzzle of a gun pointed in a safe direction.

· Never point a gun at anything you do not intend to shoot.

Once you have those three rules memorized, you're ready to learn to shoot. But it's not enough just to know the three rules of safe gun handling. You must put them into practice every time you pick up a firearm. Are you ready now? Let's begin...

Protect Your Eyes & Ears

Anytime you're planning to shoot any type of firearm, your shooting equipment should always include proper eye and hearing protection. Adequate protection need not be expensive. Some entry-level shooting glasses are very inexpensive, and hearing protection can be as cheap as a set of foam earplugs that cost less than a dollar per pair. The thing to remember is that you only get one pair of eyes and ears during your lifetime. Learn to protect them as a young shooter—every time you pick up a gun—and it will become a positive habit that you practice throughout your shooting career. Many older shooters failed to do this consistently, and now are suffering from hearing loss later in their lives. I should know, I'm one of them.

Managing Recoil

One of the first questions new shooters usually ask is, "Will the gun kick me?" What they are referring to is something known as recoil, the force at which a gun pushes up and back when it is fired. All firearms recoil, some just more than others. What determines the amount of felt recoil is the weight of a gun and the amount of gunpowder in a cartridge or shell when it's fired.

For example, a relatively lightweight gun shooting a cartridge or shell with a large amount of gunpowder will have more felt recoil than a heavier gun shooting a cartridge or shell with a light powder charge. The thing to remember that will reduce the amount of recoil you feel is to hold a firearm firmly when you shoot. If firing a rifle or shotgun, hold the gun securely with both hands and also firmly against your shoulder and side of your face. If firing a handgun, hold the gun firmly with two hands instead of just one. It is also better to begin shooting small-caliber rifles and handguns and small-gauge shotguns rather than large, as these guns have less recoil. In that way, you'll be able to get used to the feel of recoil and won't develop a "flinch" when you pull the trigger. You can then gradually work your way up to shooting guns of larger calibers or gauges.

Recoil in Bows

When shooting a bow and arrow, you should know that a bow does not recoil like a firearm. Although you will feel the bow vibrate when an arrow is released from the string, a bow does not kick up and back nearly as much as a firearm. Hold a bow firmly when you draw and release an arrow from the string, but not

You should always get into the steadiest shooting position possible when firing a rifle or handgun, such as this kneeling position.

too tightly. Holding a bow with too tight a grip could throw off the accuracy of your arrow.

Determine Your Dominant Eye

Just as most people are either right- or left-handed, most people are also either right- or left-eyed. In other words, one of your eyes is stronger than the other. This condition is called eye dominance, or your "master" eye. Most people who are right-eyed are also right-handed, and most people who are left-eyed are also left-handed. But some people are not, and that is called cross-dominance. Determining which of your eyes is your master eye is important in shooting, because your master eye must lie in line with the gun barrel for you to shoot accurately.

To shoot most accurately, your master eye should lie in line with the gun barrel. This shooter appears to have a cross-dominant problem; her master eye is her left eye, but she is attempting to shoot the gun from her right shoulder.

For example, a person who is right-eye dominant (their right eye is their master eye) should be shooting a rifle or shotgun from their right shoulder. If a shooter is left-eye dominant, he or she should be shooting a rifle or shotgun from the left shoulder. A problem occurs when a person who is right-eye dominant is left-handed. That person will try to shoot from their left shoulder, but their master eye will not lie directly in line with the gun barrel. The same is true for the shooter who is left-eye dominant but right-handed. That person will attempt to shoot from his or her right shoulder, but their master eye will not lie directly in line with the gun barrel. The result is that those shooters will be less accurate in their shooting, and could become frustrated.

There are several ways to determine which of your eyes is your master eye. Here's a simple test that you can do right where you're sitting: With both of your eyes open, extend your right arm and right index finger and point at an object across the room, say a picture hanging on the wall. Next, take your left hand and cover your left eye. Did your index finger jump off the picture? If not, you are likely right-eyed. That means that your right eye is your master or dominant eye. As a result, you should be shooting a rifle or shotgun from your right shoulder.

If your index finger did jump off the object across the room, you are likely left-eyed. Your left eye is your master or dominant eye. That means you should be shooting a rifle or shotgun from your left shoulder. To make sure which of your eyes is your master eye, try the test several times. You can also try the test with your left hand and left index finger and by covering your right eye.

Ideally, you want to be shooting from the same shoulder or side as your master eye. If you find that difficult, in other words if you are cross-dominant, there are ways around the problem. One solution is to learn to shoot from the opposite shoulder, the shoulder in line with your master eye. This may feel strange at first, like eating with the wrong hand, but you can get used to it. Another solution is to put a small piece of opaque tape over the lens of your shooting glasses in front of your master eye. This will force your weak eye—the one in line with the sight—to take over as your dominant eye when shooting. The good news is that few shooters are cross-dominant. Hopefully, you won't be one of them. If you are, you may want to consult a shooting coach to help you get started.

If your left eye is your master or stronger eye, you should be shooting from your left shoulder (as in this picture), and vice versa if you are right-eye dominant.

RIFLES & HANDGUNS

Shooting a rifle and handgun are similar for several reasons. First, both guns shoot bullets, not shot. And to shoot a bullet accurately on a rifle or handgun, a shooter must first line up the sights, usually a front and rear sight, with the target before pulling the trigger. To do this, a shooter usually completely closes or squints his off eye, the eye that is not his dominant eye. Rifles and handguns are usually fired at stationary targets.

By contrast, shooting a shotgun is very different. In shotgun shooting, a target is usually moving and the gun fires many small pellets all at the same time, not a single bullet. Most good shotgun shooters keep both eyes open when shooting. We'll talk more about shotgun shooting later, but the important thing to remember for now is that rifle and handgun shooting are similar to one another, but significantly different than shotgun shooting.

Rifles and handguns are fired from four common shooting positions: standing, kneeling, sitting, or prone (lying down). When shooting rifles or handguns, always get into the steadiest shooting position you can for the shooting or hunting situation you find yourself in. Prone is the steadiest position, because most of your body is in contact with the ground. Standing is the least steady position, because only your feet are touching the ground. Kneeling and sitting are somewhere in between the standing and prone positions in their steadiness, with sitting being steadier than kneeling.

Shooting Position

Stance is the first thing to consider when shooting a rifle from the standing position. Your feet should be about shoulder-width apart, and you should be standing at about a 90-degree angle to the target. In other words, if you shoot a rifle from your right shoulder, your left shoulder should be pointed at the target. If you shoot from your left shoulder, your right shoulder should be pointed at the target. If shooting a handgun from the standing position, a shooter usually faces the target head-on, not at an angle as when rifle shooting.

In the kneeling position for shooting rifles and handguns, one knee is on the ground and the elbow of one arm rests on your other knee, helping support the gun. In the sitting position, your rear end is on the ground with elbows on each of your knees. In the prone position for rifle shooting, your

To sight-in a rifle, move the rear sight in the direction you want the hits on the target to move.

body should be lying at about a 45-degree angle to the target. For handgun shooting from the prone position, a shooter should be facing the target.

It should be mentioned, too, that handguns can be held and fired with just one hand, but are more accurate if held and fired two-handed. Whenever possible, shoot a handgun with a two-hand grip. And always keep safety in mind. Because handguns are shorter than long guns—rifles and shotguns—they are also more dangerous. A careless twist of your wrist and you will quickly be pointing a handgun in an unsafe direction. Shooting a handgun with two hands helps you control the muzzle better than with just one hand.

Sighting-in

You can be the best rifle or handgun shooter in the world, using the best of equipment, but if your gun is not sighted-in properly, you will not hit the target. Sighting-in simply means adjusting the sights of a gun so that the bullet hits where the gun is aiming.

In sighting-in, you first need to decide at what distance you want your gun zeroed. In other words, at what distance do you want the bullet hitting the

To sight-in a rifle or handgun, move the rear sight in the same direction you want the hits on the target to move.

center of the target? For example, if the gun is a .22 caliber rifle that you want to use for small-game hunting, you might want the gun to hit dead on at 50 yards (45.7 m), possibly even closer. On the other hand, if it's a big-game rifle you're sighting-in, maybe 200 yards (182.9 m) is a better zeroing distance. To make this decision, you have to determine at what distance most of your targets will be most of the time.

You might be asking why you have to choose a zeroing distance. After all, doesn't a bullet fly in a straight line to the target? The answer to that question is no. Rifle and handgun bullets do not travel in a straight line to the target. Rather, they fly in a slight arc known as a trajectory. For illustration, we'll take a .22 rifle and

Telescopic sights, also known as scopes, have two adjustment knobs, one to move the scope side to side and one to move it up and down.

sight-in the gun for 50 yards (45.7 m). Here's how it's done.

First, tack a large paper target downrange at 50 yards (45.7 m). Make sure that the area behind the target is safe and that no ricochets can occur. Next, place the gun on a solid rest such as a shooting bench. If you aren't shooting at a range with a shooting bench, an alternative is to lie on the ground with the barrel of the gun propped on a rolled-up sleeping bag or another object with a soft surface. The idea is to make the gun as steady as possible without having the barrel touching or resting against a hard surface. If it is, the gun may "jump" slightly when fired, throwing off the accuracy of your shot.

Next, put on your shooting glasses and hearing protection. Then, taking your time, line up the sights on the rifle with the target and fire one shot. Do this a second time, then a third time, but always be slow and methodical in your shooting, never in a hurry. Notice that I didn't say shoot three shots in succession. You want to pause between shots, taking careful aim each time to make each shot as accurate as possible. Remember to squeeze the trigger, don't jerk it. And don't adjust the sights on the gun between shots.

Once you've fired three shots, unload and go downrange to check your target. If you're shooting at a public range where other shooters are firing, make sure that the range is clear and safe before walking downrange. A pair of binoculars or a spotting scope will allow you to check the hits on the target without having to walk back and forth after each set of three shots.

If you had a solid gun rest, took your time in aiming, and squeezed the trigger on each shot, the three hits on the target should be somewhat close together in what's called a group. The idea is then to adjust the sights on the gun so that the next group of three hits moves closer to the center of the target. To do this with a rifle or handgun with open sights, move the rear sight in the same direction you want the hits to move on the target. For example, if you want the group of three hits to move left, move the rear sight of the gun to the left. If you want the three hits to move right, move the rear sight of the gun to the right. If you want the hits to move up, raise the rear sight. If you want the hits to move down, lower the rear sight.

But no matter which way you move the rear sight, move it only slightly. Even a small amount of adjustment of the rear sight can move the hits on a target several inches, especially when shooting at long ranges. When sighting-in a rifle or handgun with a telescopic sight, the scope will have two adjustment knobs, one on the top of the scope and another on the side. One knob moves the hits up and down on the target and the other moves them side to side.

Continue this process of firing three shots at a time until the bullets are consistently striking the center of the target. When they are, the gun is zeroed or sighted-in for that particular distance, 50 yards (45.7 m). If shooting at distances longer than 50 yards (45.7 m) with that gun, bullets will drop slightly, meaning hit lower on the target. If shooting at closer distances than 50 yards (45.7 m) with that gun, bullets will hit slightly high on the target. Again, this drop or rise in where the bullets hit is determined by trajectory, the flight path of a bullet. If you ever want to sight-in that gun for a different distance, go through the same procedure just described, only at the desired distance.

Remember, too, that gun sights can sometimes be bumped out of alignment, throwing off the accuracy of a gun. This can happen while hunting or sometimes even while transporting a firearm. It's a good idea to occasionally check and make sure that your gun is still shooting where you are aiming by firing a group of three shots. This is especially important before going hunting, as you don't want to wound a game animal and have it get away because your gun's sights were out of alignment.

Trigger Squeeze

How you pull the trigger of a rifle or handgun is very important for accurate shooting. If you jerk the trigger when pulling it, even a little, the gun may move just enough that the bullet will be thrown off its mark. Expert shooters will tell you that a good trigger pull when shooting a rifle or handgun is actually more of a squeeze than a pull. Once you've lined up a rifle's or handgun's sights with the target and are ready to fire, you should squeeze the trigger so gently and slowly that you don't know exactly when the gun will fire. It should actually come as somewhat of a surprise to you when the gun finally goes off. Learn to shoot a rifle or handgun using this trigger-squeeze technique and you will quickly become an accurate shooter.

Another technique that will help make you an accurate shooter—a technique used by many competition rifle shooters—is a simple breathing exercise. Once you've lined up the gun's sights on the target and are ready to shoot, take a deep breath, then let it out. Next, take a second deep

To be most accurate when rifle shooting, learn to control breathing. First, take a deep breath, let it out, then take another deep breath and let it out half way before squeezing the trigger.

breath, let it half way out, hold your breath, and squeeze the trigger until the gun fires.

Through practice, you'll learn what shooting techniques work best for you. The thing to remember is to get into the steadiest position possible for the particular shooting or hunting situation you're in, then squeeze the trigger of a rifle or handgun, don't jerk it.

SHOTGUNS

Shooting a shotgun is much different from shooting a rifle or handgun. And because shotguns are different, they require different shooting techniques. Shotguns were made to shoot moving targets at relatively close ranges, out to about 40 yards (36.6 m). Usually, there is little time to aim a shotgun at a moving target, which is why there is no rear sight on a shotgun. So instead of aiming a shotgun as you would aim a rifle or handgun, shotguns are pointed. That's a very important fact and one that bears repeating: Shotguns are pointed, not aimed.

Shooting Positions

Shotguns are usually fired from a standing position. First, get into the type of stance a boxer might use. You should be facing the target with your legs about shoulder-width apart and your knees slightly bent. One foot should be a little in front of the other. If you shoot a gun from your right shoulder, your left foot should be a little forward of your right. If you shoot from your left shoulder, your right foot should be a little forward of your left. Put a little more weight on your front foot, a little less on your back foot. By facing the target and getting into this boxer-type stance, you will be able to swing a shotgun just like a boxer throws a punch. You will also be able to track a target and swing your shotgun in a semicircle, a nearly 180-degree arc in front of you. Being able to quickly swing on a target and follow through after pulling the trigger is very important in shotgun shooting.

Good shotgun shooters also keep both eyes open and on the target when shooting. You should never look at the front bead of a shotgun when tracking a target, as if attempting to aim. If you do, that may be just enough distraction to slow your swing and cause you to miss. Remember, shotguns are pointed; rifles and handguns are aimed.

Shotguns are made for shooting clay targets or moving game at relatively close ranges, out to about 40 yards.

Shotgunning Techniques

There are three basic shotgunning methods used for shooting at flying targets: instinctive, swing-through, and sustained-lead. Shotgun shooters and hunters usually settle on one of the three methods, the one that works best for them.

New shooters would do well to try the instinctive method of shotgun shooting first. Why? Because your body already knows how to instinctively track a flying target. And if it already knows, it's then just a matter of tapping in to your body's natural shooting ability, allowing your brain and reflexes to do what they instinctively already know how to do.

For example, point your finger at a moving object, such as a flying bird or a car passing along the street or road in front of your house. Did you have to stop and think about how to point? No, you just did it. Your brain and arm have pointed so many times at so many things in the past that you didn't have to think about the action or how to accomplish it. Shooting a shotgun is basically the same technique. Just think of a shotgun as an extension of your arm.

The key to hitting flying targets with a shotgun using the instinctive shooting method is simply to point and shoot. When you see a target in range, point at it with the shotgun and pull the trigger. Don't aim, and don't concern yourself with how far to lead the target. With the instinctive method of shotgun shooting, your brain automatically takes lead into account and makes the necessary adjustments. Remember, just point and shoot. It's a simple concept—one that sounds almost too good to be true—but it works. However, simple does not necessarily mean easy. Any method of shotgun shooting takes practice to learn, and the instinctive shotgun shooting method is no exception.

One last tip about learning the instinctive method of shotgun shooting: A wise shooting coach once said, "Tis better to miss with style than to hit with bad form." Why is that true? Because when you are first learning how to shoot a shotgun, you are forming habits. Form good shooting habits by using a good shooting style and the hits will come. Form bad habits and you may break a few targets, but your bad shooting habits will eventually have you missing more targets than you hit.

The swing-through method of shotgun shooting is different from the instinctive method. It involves tracking a moving target by starting the muzzle of the gun behind the target, pulling the trigger when the gun catches up to the target, and then ending the swing with a follow-through.

Follow-through in shotgun shooting is just as important as in other hand-eye coordination sports.

The sustained-lead method of shotgun shooting involves placing the muzzle of the gun in front of a moving target and keeping it there while pulling the trigger. The distance, or lead, you keep the gun in front of the target is determined by how far the target is from the shooter and how fast it's moving. The theory behind this shooting method is that the moving target then flies into the string of shotgun pellets.

As a new or young shooter, try all three methods of shotgun shooting techniques—instinctive, swing-through, and sustained-lead—to see which one works best for you. Once you know which one does, it's then just a matter of practice to become a better shot. Shoot more, shoot often, and your shooting skills are bound to improve.

Trigger Pull

Just as shooting a shotgun is different from shooting a rifle or handgun, so is the trigger pull. Or at least it should be. Earlier in this chapter we learned that the trigger pull of a rifle or handgun is really more of a squeeze, not a pull. When shooting a shotgun, the trigger pull is just the opposite of that used for

Similar to shooting a rifle, an archer should stand at a 90-degree angle to the target with feet about shoulder-width apart.

a rifle or handgun; it should be more of a quick jerk or a "slap." The reason is that when shooting at moving targets you don't have time to squeeze a trigger. When a clay target or game animal is within range and you decide to shoot, pull the trigger of a shotgun quickly and firmly, don't hesitate.

BOWS & ARROWS

Learning to become a good shot with a bow and arrow begins with a good stance. In the same way as when shooting a rifle from a standing position, stand at a 90-degree angle to the target with your feet about a shoulder-width apart. If a shooter is right-handed, he will grasp the grip of the bow in his left hand and his right hand will pull the bowstring. Just the opposite is true for a left-handed shooter.

Place an arrow on the bowstring—called nocking an arrow—and grasp the bowstring with your middle three fingers. Your index finger should be above the nocked arrow and your middle and ring fingers should be below. The string should lie in the first crease or joint nearest the tip of your fingers. Draw the bow by pushing it away from you with your bow hand and pulling the bowstring toward you with the three fingers on your string hand.

At full draw, your string hand should come to a location on your face called the anchor point. Some archers anchor to the corner of their mouth while others anchor under their chin or another location on their face. The idea is to anchor to the same location before every shot. Doing so makes your shots as accurate as possible.

Once anchored, line up the sights on your bow with the target, pause, and release the arrow by relaxing your three fingers holding the bowstring. Once the arrow is released, hold the bow in place until the arrow hits the target. This is called follow-through, and it is just as important in shooting a bow and arrow as it is in shooting firearms.

Shooting a crossbow is more like shooting a rifle than a bow because a crossbow has a stock attached. After pulling back the bowstring on a crossbow—called cocking—nock an arrow on the bowstring and then line up the sights of the crossbow with the target. To release an arrow from a crossbow, push the crossbow's safety button to the "Off" or "Fire" position and squeeze the trigger, just like when shooting a rifle. And just like when shooting a bow, remember to follow-through by holding a crossbow in position until the arrow hits the target.

Follow-through in archery is just as important as when shooting firearms. Once you release an arrow, remember to hold the bow in place until the arrow hits the target.

chapter 4

SHOOTING PRACTICE

Part of the fun of shooting is trying new shooting games. Whether shooting guns or bows and arrows, all of the games will test your skills and make you a better shot. Who knows, maybe you'll become such a good marksman that you'll want to start competing on a shooting team. Many high schools across the country have shooting teams and shooting programs, both for riflery and shotgunning. Some universities even offer scholarships to exceptional shooters that could help pay for part of your college education.

RIFLES & HANDGUNS

Plinking is the name given to shooting a rifle or handgun informally just for fun, such as getting together with friends to shoot a few aluminum soda cans or plastic water jugs. Rifles and handguns in .22-caliber are popular for plinking, because their ammunition is inexpensive and the guns have almost no recoil.

Metal silhouette shooting is a more formal kind of rifle and handgun shooting, usually using high-caliber guns. The targets in this game are steel plates that have been cut into various shapes—circles, squares, or the outlines of game animals—and mounted on hinges. When a target is hit by a bullet, you hear a distinctive "tink" sound as the bullet strikes the metal plate, but the target only counts as a hit if it tips over backwards. Metal silhouette shooting can take place at close distances, such as only a few feet (meters) away from the targets, as when shooting handguns, or at many hundreds of yards (kilometers), as when shooting high-powered rifles with scopes.

A type of metal silhouette shooting is even an official Winter Olympics event: biathlon. Shooters on cross-country skis, with a rifle on a sling over their back, ski from shooting station to shooting station as fast as possible. Upon arriving at a station, they pull the rifle from their back, quickly lie down on the ground in a prone shooting position, and then must shoot several metal silhouette targets, knocking each over before skiing on to the next shooting station. Biathlon is a physically grueling event, one that takes not

A prone position (lying down) is the most stable rifle shooting position, because your entire body is in contact with the ground.

only being a good shot but also being in great shape. The sport was developed years ago by hunters in northern Europe who hunted from skis.

Cowboy action shooting is a relatively new shooting game, having become popular in the last decade or so. Participants dress up like cowboys—even taking on western nicknames—and shoot single-action handguns, lever-action rifles, and hinge-action shotguns. The guns are replicas of those used in the Old West, usually models from the late 19th or early 20th century. All kinds of various competitions have been developed for and by cowboy action shooters, and attending such an event, even if you don't go to shoot, is a lot of fun and a history lesson all at the same time.

SHOTGUNS

Trapshooting (or "trap") is the oldest of the shotgun shooting games. The game gets its name from live-pigeon shooting contests of the past. Years ago, a bird was held in a box or "trap" and released on command of the shooter. The object of the competition was to shoot the pigeon as it attempted to fly away, but the bird only counted as a score if it fell within a large circle marked on the ground surrounding the trap. As pigeons became shorter in supply and public opinion turned against using live birds as targets, "clay pigeons" were developed. These eventually evolved into the clay targets used today in trapshooting and other shotgun sports.

Trapshooting is also one of the simplest of the shotgun shooting sports, yet not easily mastered. A machine for throwing clay targets is mounted in a small house dug partially into the ground in front of five shooting positions called stations or posts. Targets are thrown away from shooters either singly or in pairs, depending upon the particular trap game being played. Each target is launched in a different and random direction from the previous target, so shooters are never quite sure which angle the next target will take.

Trapshooters stand anywhere from 16 to 27 yards (14.6 to 24.7 m) behind the trap house, depending upon their skill level. Five shooters (one on each of the five stations) make up a full trap squad. Station number one shooter begins the round by calling for a target using the word "Pull!" The target is immediately launched from the trap house by an electrical pulse, either by the manual push of a button or by an acoustic-release device that uses the shooter's voice to trigger the trap.

A good shotgunner faces the target with her stance, as this young shooter has learned.

With the instinctive method of shotgun shooting there is no need to consciously lead a target, just point and shoot.

The shooter fires at the target and a scorekeeper records the result, either a hit or miss. A target is considered hit if even a small piece can be detected flying from it. It is then shooter number two's turn to fire, and so on down the line. Once all shooters have each fired five shots, they rotate to the next shooting station. After the shooters have fired five shells at each station the round is complete. A perfect score for a round of trap is 25 hits.

In trapshooting, clay targets are thrown away from shooters. In the game of skeet, targets fly mostly side to side.

Skeet is similar to trap, but the game differs in that shooters are shooting at clay targets crossing in front of them rather than flying away. Also, there are two houses throwing targets in skeet shooting, instead of just one as in trapshooting. A high target house is to the left of a skeet shooter and 10 feet (3.1 m) off the ground. A low target house is to the right of the shooter and 3 feet (.9 m) from the ground. In a round of skeet, a shooter fires from eight positions laid out in a semi-circle between the two target houses. Shooters call for a target using the same word as in trapshooting: "Pull!" In the game of skeet, either one or two clay targets are thrown at a time. Shooting distances are closer in skeet than in trapshooting, but target angles are sharper, making a smooth, quick gun swing important. As in trapshooting, a perfect score for a round of skeet is 25 hits.

Sporting clays is a shooting game very different from trap and skeet, and is sometimes described as "golf with a shotgun." While trap and skeet fields are well defined and laid out over a relatively small shooting area, a sporting clays range can sprawl over many acres (hectares). Anywhere from 10 to 18 shooting stations make up a sporting clays range. And unlike trap and skeet, where you know that targets will fly at certain angles and certain speeds, sporting clays targets are thrown at a variety of angles and speeds. At any one station you may be shooting at single targets, true doubles (two targets thrown at the same time), or "report" doubles, where the second target is not thrown until you fire your first shot.

The original idea of sporting clays was to create a shooting game similar to the actual shots taken while hunting different game animals with a shotgun: quail, grouse, pheasants, ducks, and geese. Most sporting clays courses even have some clay targets that bounce along the ground, known as "rabbits." A round of sporting clays consists of shooting either 50 or 100 shells. A type of sporting clays, known as five-stand sporting, can be set up and shot on a regular trap or skeet field.

"Plinking" is getting together with a few friends to shoot soda cans or plastic milk jugs, usually with a .22.

Annie Oakley is a fun shotgun shooting game to play when casually shooting clay targets with friends. The game is named after the famous woman sharpshooter of the late 19th and early 20th centuries, and can be played with as few as three shooters. Here's how it's done. As many shooters as want to play step up to the shooting line standing side by side. The first three shooters load their shotguns with one shell each. Shooter number one calls for a clay target, and if he shoots and breaks it, he's still in the game. If he misses, shooter number two shoots at the same target, and if he breaks it, he puts shooter number one out of the game. If shooter number two misses, shooter number three gets a chance to shoot at the same target, and if he hits it he puts both shooter one and shooter two out of the game. The game proceeds down the line, three shooters at a time, until only one shooter is left. This is a fun game to play with shotgun shooters of various ages and skill levels, as anyone can get lucky and put anyone else out of the game.

BOWFISHING

Bowfishing is a great way to keep your bow shooting skills honed during the summer months. Most states and provinces allow rough fish—carp, gar, etc.—to be taken with bows and arrows. But bowfishing requires some specialized equipment, such as a fish arrow with a barbed tip. The fish arrow is attached to a stout cord that is wound around a large reel. The reel attaches to the bow. When a fish arrow is released, it pulls the cord with it. If a fish is struck, the barb on the arrow keeps the arrow from pulling out of the fish. The shooter then lands the fish by pulling in the cord, hand over hand.

Bowfishing is a lot of fun, and some really big fish have been taken by bow and arrow, some weighing more than 50 pounds (22.7 kg). Sometimes bowfishing can be especially productive at night, as larger fish move closer to shore in the dark. But be especially careful if bowfishing at night. Make sure of your target before releasing an arrow, and never go bowfishing at night alone.

Indoor archery ranges are very popular with many bowhunters during the winter. They are a fun way to keep your bow-shooting skills sharp by shooting regularly, once per week or so. Indoor ranges vary in size and sophistication. For example, an indoor range could be as simple as a few hay bales set up in a barn, or possibly a sportsmen's club that uses its clubhouse one night per week for bow shooting. But many larger cities today have dedicated indoor archery

Once you can group arrows this tightly from at least 20 yards away, you may be ready to try bowhunting.

Shooting a bow and arrows can be just as much fun as shooting firearms, and you only have to buy the ammunition once!

ranges with all the amenities. Shooters usually pay by the hour to use these facilities, or have a membership, and most of these ranges have an archery pro shop on site where shooters can buy bows, arrows, and archery accessories. These ranges are great places to "try-before-you-buy," as most will have various kinds of bows and arrows available that shooters of all skill levels can use. They're also great places to get advice about fine-tuning your archery equipment and to learn advanced shooting techniques from true professionals.

Three dimensional (3-D) archery courses are fun to try during warmer months. If you are familiar with sporting clays ranges for shotgun shooters, 3-D archery is similar. Full-body, foam archery targets molded in the shape of game animals are placed at various distances throughout a woodland setting. And as with sporting clays, archers walk from shooting station to shooting station where they must guess the various target distances, then take their best shot. If they misjudge the distance to a target, their arrow flies either too short or long. This is good practice, because during an actual bowhunting situation, misjudging the distance to an animal means missing. Worse yet, misjudging distance and making a bad hit on a game animal could wound it and have it get away injured.

In recent years, 3-D archery shooting has become so popular that tournament circuits have sprung up. But even if you don't have a 3-D archery range near you, shooting at a single 3-D target, such as a foam deer, is better practice for hunting than shooting at paper targets. Why? Because shooting at a full-body target causes you to focus on placing your arrows in the vital heart/lung area of an animal for a killing shot. Practice shooting with 3-D targets can pay big dividends during actual hunting situations.

Shooting at a foam animal target is better practice for bowhunting than shooting at paper archery targets, as it forces you to concentrate on placing your arrow in the vital heart/lung area.

Hunting is not for everyone, but once you become a proficient shot with firearms or archery equipment you may want to give it a try.

chapter 5

GETTING STARTED IN HUNTING

Hunting is not for everyone. But once you become a safe, competent shooter, you may want to give hunting a try. For many sportsmen and women, hunting is a fun, fulfilling adventure like no other—an activity that will challenge your outdoor skills for a lifetime. And for some people, hunting even becomes a lifestyle: They eat, sleep, and breathe hunting every day of the year. Some even become professional hunters.

Just keep in mind that if you choose to learn to hunt, you are taking on an even higher responsibility than you did when learning to shoot. Why? The reason is that when hunting you will be killing game animals—taking an animal's life. That is a serious responsibility, and something that should not be entered into lightly or in a joking manner. Respecting the game animals you hunt is primary. That's why it's important to become a good shot, so that you can make a clean, safe, humane kill every time you pull the trigger or release an arrow.

By far, the easiest way to learn to hunt is by first hunting with a mentor. A mentor is someone who is older and more experienced than you, usually an adult. If your father, mother, uncle, or family friend is a hunter, that person would be a natural choice to teach you how to hunt. Or maybe you have a friend about your age whose father or mother hunts; could you ask them to teach you?

But what if you don't know anyone who hunts. What do you do then? In most parts of the country, sportsmen's clubs are available. These are groups of men and women who meet regularly to target shoot, talk hunting, and do volunteer wildlife conservation projects. If you don't have someone to teach you to hunt, contact any of the sportsmen's clubs in your area and ask them if they have a young hunter mentoring program. Or, another way to contact a mentor would be through a hunter-education course instructor.

HUNTER EDUCATION COURSES

In all U.S. states and Canadian provinces, it is now mandatory that all young hunters complete a certified hunter education course before purchasing a regular hunting license. This regulation is not only a good idea for safety's sake, but the course is also fun. Depending upon where you live, a hunter education course could be held over a period of several evenings or last as long as a full day or more. Home-study hunter education courses are also available.

No matter how you choose to take the course, you'll learn about such things as firearms and ammunition, bows and arrows, safe gun and bow handling, shooting and hunting techniques, wildlife conservation, wilderness safety and survival tips, game care, and a variety of other topics. To find out the specific details and requirements for a hunter education course in your area, contact your state or provincial wildlife agency, or go online to the International Hunter Education Association Web site, http://www.ihea.com.

Some states now have an apprentice hunting license program that allows young people or other first-time hunters to try hunting before actually completing a hunter education course. However, the young apprentice hunter must be accompanied in the field by a licensed, adult hunter. To find out if your state or province has such a program, contact the wildlife agency in your area.

Some states also have special youth hunting seasons that take place prior to regular hunting seasons, so check those out, too. These special seasons give kids a crack at hunting certain game animals or hunting on certain special areas before the general hunting public is permitted.

Be sure you know the regulations that apply in your state or province for the season and species you choose to pursue.

Patterning your shotgun prior to the hunting season is important in wild turkey hunting. A good turkey gun should place half a dozen pellets into a turkey's vital head/neck area.

PURCHASING YOUR FIRST FIREARM

Buying your first gun is a big step and one that should not be taken lightly. Firearms can be expensive, and you don't want to invest in the wrong type of gun. With some online research and a little homework, you can find a gun that will provide a lifetime of dependable service.

The first step is to decide what type of shooting or hunting you will be doing most. Will you be mainly target shooting or hunting? And if hunting, will you be hunting mostly small game or big game? Those questions can only be answered by you, the shooter.

In general, a new shooter or hunter living in most areas of North America would do well to purchase a 20-gauge shotgun or .22 caliber rifle as his or her first gun. Most 20-gauge shotguns are lighter than their 12-gauge big brothers, but can be used to hunt most of the same game types. A 20-gauge shotgun can also be loaded with deer slugs to hunt big game. Overall, a 20-gauge is a good all-around choice for a first shotgun. Likewise, a .22 caliber is a good all-

A single-shot shotgun, such as a 20-gauge, would be a good choice as a first gun for most young shooters and hunters.

around choice for your first rifle. Most .22s are lightweight, their ammunition is inexpensive to purchase, they produce almost no recoil, and they can be used to hunt small game.

The final question in purchasing a firearm is whether to buy a new or used gun. Used guns are less expensive, but before putting your money down on a used firearm, make sure that the gun you are considering is in good condition and safe working order. If in doubt, ask the seller if you can take the gun to a gunsmith for an appraisal. If the seller refuses, walk away from the deal. There are many, many good used guns on the market, so don't be in too big of a hurry to buy.

The advantage of buying a new firearm rather than a used one is that you know the gun is in safe working order and that you have a guarantee to back up your purchase. All new firearms will also come with an instruction manual, while most used guns do not. Finally, when buying your first gun, don't forget to also purchase a transport case—these can be either soft or hard-sided—and a gun-cleaning kit. And if you don't have a lockable gun safe at home for storage, purchase a trigger lock for your gun.

PURCHASING YOUR FIRST BOW & ARROWS

Becoming an accomplished bow-hunter is even more difficult than becoming a good gun hunter. Why? Because a bowhunter must get very close to a game animal to make a killing shot. For example, most deer killed by bowhunters are shot at distances of less than 20 yards (18.3 m). To get that close to a deer, or any species of game animal, requires excellent woodsmanship and hunting skills. If that kind of challenge appeals to you, you may enjoy bowhunting.

Purchasing your first bow and arrows is similar to purchasing a firearm. Do you buy new or used? There are advantages and disadvantages both ways.

When choosing a bow, the draw weight must be light enough to easily pull back and hold at full draw; at the same time the bow must have sufficient draw weight to propel an arrow with enough energy to penetrate the body of a big-game animal and kill it. The very minimum bow draw weight for accomplishing this is about 40 pounds (18.2 kg). When hunting big game, you should use a bow with the heaviest draw weight you can comfortably pull and hold at full draw. As your body grows and your muscles become stronger, you will be able to increase the draw weight of the bow you shoot.

Unlike compound, recurve, and longbows, crossbows aren't held at full draw by the shooter. However, they still must be drawn or cocked by the shooter. Make sure that when choosing a crossbow for hunting you can bring it to full draw easily and safely. If you need to use a cocking device to do so, use one. Once a crossbow is fully drawn, don't forget to push the safety button to "On" or "Safe," and leave it there until just before you are ready to shoot. You should never walk around the woods or sit in a hunting blind holding a crossbow with the safety button in the "Off" or "Fire" position. As when shooting or hunting with a firearm, the only time a crossbow's safety button is pushed to the "Off" or "Fire" position is just before you are ready to shoot.

Keep in mind, too, that arrows must match the particular bow with which you choose to hunt. There are also many different broadheads on the market used for tipping arrows and hunting big game. Some broadheads have movable blades, while others have fixed blades. Various broadhead brands also differ in weight. Try several different broadheads on your arrows to see which ones

Fletching on an arrow helps stabilize it in flight, making the arrow more accurate.

shoot best with your bow. A good place to begin your research about broadheads is at a professional archery shop.

As a new or young bowhunter considering buying your first bow, should you choose a compound bow, recurve bow, longbow, or crossbow? Here are a few things to consider in making that decision. First, a compound bow has let-off. Let-off simply means that the shooter is holding less draw weight at full draw than he would be if hunting with a recurve bow or longbow. For a new or young hunter, the let-off feature of a compound bow is a significant advantage.

Another good choice for a first bow, if legal for hunting in your area, is a crossbow. An advantage of hunting with a crossbow is that the string isn't held at full draw by the shooter. Instead, the string is held at full draw by the bow itself. This allows a crossbow to be drawn long before a game animal appears within range, eliminating that crucial decision every new bowhunter has to learn to make—when to draw. Many game animals have been spooked by inexperienced bowhunters drawing their bow at the wrong time, giving away their position.

So once you've decided which kind of bow to buy, the decision then becomes much like purchasing a firearm—do you buy new or used? And as with purchasing a firearm, new and used bows have both advantages and disadvantages. Used bows are usually less costly than buying new, but new bows come with a manufacturer's guarantee should anything go wrong. A professional bow shop can help get you started in your search for a quality hunting bow.

WHERE TO HUNT: PUBLIC VS. PRIVATE LAND

Unless you have the money and time to travel long distances, the question of where to hunt will largely be determined by where you live. For example, in much of the eastern United States, most hunting takes place on private land because there is relatively little public land available. In the western United States, however, just the opposite is true. Vast areas of the West—millions of acres of national forests, national grasslands, and other areas—are publicly owned and open to hunters. In many areas of the West it is possible to hunt all day, or several days, and never even see another hunter. But no matter where you choose to hunt, on public or private land, it is the responsibility of the hunter to always know exactly where he or she is while in the field, and that it is legal to hunt on that location.

Learning to hunt from a mentor—an older, more experienced hunter—is the best way to get started in the hunting field.

The Internet can be a great place to begin researching a new hunting area. Web sites such as http://www.googleearth.com allow you to see a hunting area online before you ever actually arrive in person. Other good places to research new hunting areas online include state and provincial Department of Natural Resources Web sites, hunting Web sites, and chat rooms.

Getting Permission to Hunt from Landowners

Some of the best hunting in North America occurs on private property, but you cannot legally hunt on those lands until you've first obtained permission to do so from the landowner. In some areas, getting permission may be as

You must have permission from the landowner before hunting on private property.

simple as knocking on a farmer's door and asking to hunt. But other private lands are owned by corporations, which might require making your request to hunt in writing through a regional or corporate office.

To tip the odds in your favor of a landowner saying yes, begin well in advance of the hunting seasons. Farmers, for instance, don't appreciate being bothered during fall harvest time by hunters casually stopping by asking permission to hunt. But if you approach them during late summer, when farmers are less busy, your chances of getting a yes are much improved. And since they then will likely have more time to talk, they just may tell you the best places on their property to find game. Remember that common courtesy and good manners go a long way toward getting the answer you want. Think about how you would want someone approaching you if you were a landowner, and do the same for them.

After the hunting seasons are over, it's always a good idea to get back in touch with the landowners on whose land you hunted to thank them. This "thank-you" could be as simple as sending a Christmas card or stopping by with a small gift, such as a plate of homemade cookies. Another good idea is to offer the landowner some of your game. Always have the game cleaned, wrapped, and ready for the freezer when you make the offer. Again, remembering to say thanks will get you welcomed back to hunt next year, especially if you've treated the landowner's property as you would your own.

And along those lines, it should go without saying that if given the privilege to hunt on private land you do not leave litter lying around, even small things such as empty shotgun shells or rifle casings. You should also park your vehicle where the landowner tells you, and never drive across private property unless the landowner says it's okay. Always remember, too, that you are a guest of the landowner and hunting on private property is a privilege, not a right. Keep these things in mind, and you will likely be welcomed back on the property for years to come.

PHYSICAL FITNESS

You don't have to be big, strong, or muscular to be a hunter, but you do have to be physically fit. An upland-game hunter, for example, may walk many miles during a day's hunt in search of grouse, pheasants, quail, or rabbits. A big-game hunter may have to drag a deer or carry a quarter of an elk hundreds of yards (meters) to a vehicle or hunting camp. So before going hunting, ask yourself honestly, "What kind of physical shape am I in? How far can I run or walk without tiring? How many pull-ups, chin-ups, sit-ups, and other strength exercises can I do in a row?" If your answers to those questions are less than what you think they should be, take the time to get in shape before the hunting seasons begin. If you do, you'll not only enjoy your days afield more, but you'll be able to spend more hours in the field on any particular hunting day.

What if you're physically challenged in some way—in a wheelchair, missing a limb, or in some other way incapacitated—can you still be a hunter? Absolutely! Many hunting clubs and wildlife conservation groups take physically-challenged people hunting every year. Some state fish and wildlife agencies even provide special facilities for physically-challenged hunters, such as hunting blinds that accommodate wheel chairs.

You can even go hunting if you're blind. Don't laugh, it's true. I have a friend who was a hunter before he became blind due to complications from diabetes. But he enjoyed hunting so much that he didn't want to give up the sport just because he couldn't see. To get around his problem, he had a buddy mount a round, 6-inch-long (15.2 cm) piece of plastic PVC pipe on the

The western U.S. and Canada have millions of acres of public lands open to hunters, free of charge.

top of the stock of his shotgun. By standing behind my blind hunter friend when he shouldered his shotgun, a sighted person could look through the open piece of plastic pipe and tell him to adjust his aim either up, down, left, or right. Once on target, the blind hunter was then instructed when to shoot. Using this method, I once helped my friend bag two rabbits during an afternoon's hunt. Not bad for a blind guy, huh?

WHAT TO HUNT: SMALL VS. BIG GAME

The question of whether a new hunter should learn to hunt by first hunting small-game or big-game animals is one that cannot easily be answered the same for everyone. For example, depending upon where you live, there may be more big-game animals than small, or vice versa. And if you learn to hunt with a mentor, your mentor may have a favorite animal that he or she likes to hunt, which means you will most likely learn about hunting that animal first. In general, if you have a choice as to whether to hunt small game or big game, learning to hunt small game first has several advantages.

First, small-game hunting will give you more shooting opportunities. Most new hunters are eager to pull the trigger on a game animal, and hunting species such as rabbits, squirrels, doves, or other small game can give you several if not many shooting opportunities during a single day's hunt. By contrast, when hunting big game you may get a chance to shoot only a few times during the entire hunting

Year-round practice is required to keep your shooting skills sharp with a bow and arrow.

season. Hunting small game also gives you practice field dressing and cleaning small animals. That experience will be very helpful when the time comes to field dress and clean a big-game animal, as you will have had some practice, gained experience, and will do a better job.

So, big game or small? The choice is yours. You'll have to answer that question for yourself, taking into account the hunting opportunities in your particular part of the country and possibly the particular expertise of your hunting mentor.

Choose the Right Gun & Ammunition

What gun and ammunition to use when hunting particular game animals is an important decision and another question not easily answered. This is where a hunting mentor can help guide you. In general, shotguns and small-caliber rifles, such as .22s, are usually used for hunting small-game animals such as rabbits and squirrels. High-powered rifles are usually used for hunting big-game animals, such as deer, elk, and bears.

The biggest mistake most new gun hunters make is attempting to shoot or hunt with a firearm that does not fit them well. A gun that is too long or too heavy will not only be uncomfortable to carry in the field, but will likely result in increased recoil or "kick." Ideally, you want a gun with a stock that has been cut down to fit a young person, you in particular. "Youth-model" shotguns are built to fit kids, teens, and smaller adults. Some of these guns are even adjustable, so that as a young person's body grows the stock of the gun can be adjusted to continually fit the shooter properly.

Proper gun fit is especially important when hunting with a shotgun. If you try to shoot a shotgun that does not fit you well, you probably won't have

Pre-season scouting before hunting big-game is not only extremely important for your best chance at success, but also fun.

much success hitting your target and will eventually become frustrated. This same concept of proper gun fit applies to rifles, but is not quite as critical. A rifle hunter usually has a little more time to line up the sights on a game animal and pull the trigger, as opposed to when hunting with a shotgun.

For the proper size shot to use when hunting with a shotgun for different game animals, and for the proper size bullet to use when shooting a high-powered rifle for particular big-game animals, check with the bullet or shell manufacturer, or contact your local outdoors store.

HUNTING SMALL GAME: ZONES OF FIRE

When hunting in a group for small game, hunters are usually spread 30 to 40 yards (27.4 to 36.6 m) apart, about the distance of effective shotgun range. To be safe in such hunting situations, keep in mind something called Zones of Fire. Zones of Fire are an imaginary zone surrounding you and the other hunters in your party in which you can safely shoot, should a game animal present itself for a shot.

CHOOSING SHOT FOR SMALL-GAME HUNTING

It's important to match the right size shot with the kind of small-game hunting you will be doing. If shot pellets are too small or too large for a particular game animal, they will not be as effective as they could be, possibly resulting in a wounded animal that gets away only to suffer and die later. The following chart is a guide to helping you choose the correct size shot for small-game hunting.

Game Animal	Lead Shot Size Options
Turkey	4, 5, 6, 7½
Pheasant	4, 5, 6, 7½
Grouse	5, 6, 7½, 8
Quail	7½, 8, 9
Dove	7½, 8, 9
Woodcock, Rail, Snipe	7½, 8, 9
Rabbit	4, 5, 6, 7½
Squirrel	4, 5, 6, 7½
Ducks	1, 2, 3, 4, 5, 6, BB (all sizes listed for ducks are nontoxic shot)
Geese	1, T, BB, BBB (all sizes listed for geese are nontoxic shot)

Some states have youth hunting seasons that allow young people to hunt with a licensed, non-hunting adult before the regular hunting seasons begin.

Here's how it works: Imagine you and a group of other hunters are moving across a field walking abreast. Envision a cone-shaped area extending in front of you, with you standing at the point of the cone. That cone is your safe zone of fire. Should a game animal, such as a pheasant, flush and fly into this cone-shaped zone, you have a safe shot. But once the pheasant flies out of the cone and into the zone of fire of the hunter beside you, you no longer have a safe shot, so should not shoot. Your safe zone of fire stops at about a 45-degree angle in front of the hunter beside you. You should never swing your shotgun into another hunter's safe zone of fire. The number one cause of hunting accidents is shooters swinging on game and hitting another hunter with their shot in the process.

This same safe zone of fire extends behind you as well as in front. For instance, if a pheasant were to flush and fly back through the line of hunters, which sometimes happens, you can turn and still make a safe shot. But how you turn is very important. You never want to swing the muzzle of your gun so that it covers the hunter beside you. The safe way to make a shot behind you is to turn with the muzzle of your gun pointed up, then bring the muzzle of the gun down and take the shot.

Hunters on the two ends of the line also have a safe shot to their right or left, depending upon which end of the line they're on. It's a good idea to change places in line from time to time so that each hunter gets roughly the same amount of shooting opportunities during a day's hunt.

Another thing to remember about zones of fire for small-game hunting is to always stay in line with the other hunters in your party—don't get too far ahead or too far behind—and always know the location of all the others in your hunting party. Wearing blaze orange helps hunters keep track of one another in the field. A good rule of thumb is if you have any doubt about a shot, don't shoot. Remember, once you pull the trigger you can never call those shot pellets back. Whatever damage is done is done forever. It's always better to be safe than sorry.

Zones of fire can also apply when hunting big game. If hunting deer, for example, you should know exactly where others in your party are at all times. Again, if you have any doubt about taking a shot, don't. No deer or other game animal is worth risking an injury. Many safe shots present themselves while hunting big game or small, you just have to know which shots are safe to take and which aren't. Experience will teach you which is which.

HUNTING BIG GAME FROM TREE STANDS

Most bowhunters, and many gun hunters today, choose to hunt big game from tree stands. These elevated perches have several advantages over hunting on the ground. Tree stands allow you to see game approaching from longer distances and also allow you to safely shoot at down angles. And by a hunter being off the ground, game animals have a harder time detecting your human presence in the woods. Big-game animals also can't see you as readily when you're in a tree, and most of your human scent will be above them. That's the good news.

The bad news is that each year more hunting accidents happen because of hunters falling from tree stands than any other type of serious hunting injury. Every hunting season hunters fall from tree stands and break their arms, their legs, their necks, or become paralyzed by landing on their heads. Some hunters have even died as the result of an accidental fall from a tree stand. If you choose to hunt from a tree stand, always wear a safety belt that's secured to the tree trunk. Wearing a full body harness, one that passes between your legs and over your shoulders, is

Hunting from a tree stand can be productive, but can also be dangerous. Always wear a safety belt or full-body harness when hunting from a tree.

an even better idea. In addition to preventing you from suffering a nasty fall, wearing a safety belt or body harness is an advantage in another way. When hunting from a tree stand, a belt or harness allows you to lean out from the stand for a vertical shot, should one present itself.

Another consideration about hunting from tree stands is how to get your gun or bow safely up into the stand and then back down on the ground at the end of the hunt. To do this, don't attempt to climb with your gun or bow in your hands. Instead, tie a stout string—a parachute cord works well for this— onto your gun or bow, then tie the other end of the string around your waist or onto your belt. Leave your gun or bow on the ground, climb into the tree stand, then raise the gun or bow up to you by pulling on the string. It should go without saying that a firearm or crossbow should be unloaded when doing this. At the end of a hunt, unload your gun or crossbow and lower it to the ground before climbing out of your tree stand.

Regulations pertaining to the use of tree stands for hunting vary by state and province, so always know what you may legally do or not do in your area. And always ask permission of the landowner before putting up a tree stand on private property or using screw-in type tree steps. Hunting on public land will also have specific regulations pertaining to tree stands, so make sure you are aware of the rules and abide by them.

One final caution about tree stands. If you leave a tree stand in the woods during the hunting season, as many hunters do, it's a good idea to chain and lock it to a tree. Quite a few tree stands have been known to walk out of the woods by themselves—in other words, they were stolen. Don't take a chance. Lock your stand to a tree so that it will be there the next time you want to hunt.

HOW TO DRESS FOR HUNTING

There are so many different types of hunting throughout so many different North American environments and habitats that it is difficult to describe how a hunter should dress. No one set of hunting clothes can cover all situations. The main thing to remember is to layer your clothing so that you can take clothes off or put them back on as conditions in the field change. Keep in mind that you can't put on clothing that you don't have with you, so it's better to dress a little on the warm side.

Small-Game Hunting

Upland game hunting (game birds and other small-game animals like grouse, quail, and rabbit) is usually done by a group of several hunters, spaced about 20 to 30 yards (18.3 to 27.4 m) apart, moving abreast through cover in a loose line. When a game bird or game animal flushes, the hunter nearest the flush with a safe shot takes it. Because upland hunters are constantly on the move, they usually dress relatively lightly. A long-sleeved shirt over a T-shirt, covered by a light, blaze orange hunting jacket or hunting vest is usually all that is needed on the upper body. A pair of brush pants or briar chaps over jeans is worn over the legs. A pair of uninsulated, light field boots, either leather or a combination of rubber bottoms with leather uppers, is preferred by most upland hunters. A light pair of uninsulated shooting gloves may be needed during cooler days, and will also protect your hands from briars. Shooting

Wearing plenty of blaze orange outer clothing is a good idea while upland or big-game hunting.

gloves can also come in handy during warm weather, as they help you grip your gun if the palms of your hands tend to sweat. Most upland hunters top off their gear with a blaze orange, baseball-style cap.

Most waterfowl hunting is done from a stationary position, usually in some kind of blind, and usually during cold weather. Consequently, dressing for waterfowl hunting is very different from dressing for upland game hunting. When dressing for hunting ducks and geese, think waterproof and wear multiple layers of clothing.

Most waterfowl hunters first slip on a pair of insulated underwear and two pairs of insulated socks, topped

Wild turkey and waterfowl hunters usually dress in camouflage.

Telescopic sights, also known as scopes, magnify the target, but also magnify any movement made by the shooter.

off by multiple layers of clothing. A turtleneck sweater or shirt is a good idea, too, as it keeps the cold winds from blowing down your neck. Your outer layer should be waterproof and have a hood. Most duck and goose hunting is done on or near water, and some of the best shooting occurs on nasty weather days. When rain, sleet, or snow blows sideways as big weather fronts approach, ducks and geese begin to fly. But if you're cold, wet, and shivering, you won't be able to enjoy the action much, let alone shoot well. Good waterfowl hunting clothing is not cheap, but is worth the extra cost if you plan to be a serious duck or goose hunter.

To top off their field clothes, most waterfowl hunters also wear either a pair of insulated chest waders or hip boots. Insulated, waterproof gloves and an insulated camouflage hat that covers your ears are also necessary. Make sure that your outer layer of clothing is not only waterproof but also has some type of camouflage pattern, usually matched to the particular cover in which you'll be hunting.

Big-Game Hunting

Most big-game hunting, like waterfowl hunting, occurs during cold weather. The main difference is that you'll likely not be around as much water as when waterfowling. Nevertheless, big-game hunting can get mighty cold, as most successful hunters hunt from a ground blind or tree stand, and either way you will not be moving around much.

As in dressing for waterfowl hunting, begin with a pair of insulated underwear and two pairs of insulated socks, topped by multiple layers of clothing. The trick when walking to your hunting stand is not to have so many clothes on that you get too warm. If you do, you'll begin to sweat, which makes your inner clothing wet, which in turn eventually makes you cold. Depending upon how far you have to walk to your hunting stand, it might be a good idea to carry your outer layer or two of clothing in a backpack. Learn to stay dry, and you'll stay warmer longer.

A quality pair of insulated hunting boots is a necessity for big-game hunters. There are many brands and styles on the market offering various amounts of insulation. You'll have to determine what pair of boots is right for where you hunt. You may have to pay a little extra for waterproof yet "breathable" boots (Gore-Tex), but they're worth the cost. Insulated gloves, an insulated hat that covers your ears, and a waterproof outer shell in case it rains or snows are also needed. Most states and provinces have blaze orange clothing requirements for big-game hunting, so make sure you read the regulations.

BASIC SURVIVAL SKILLS

Every hunter should know how to survive in the wild, as those skills and knowledge could someday save your life. At a minimum, you should be able to build a fire outdoors and construct a basic shelter. Carrying a small fanny pack

Every hunter should have basic survival skills and know how to navigate through backcountry.

Every hunter should carry water, stick matches, a signaling mirror, whistle, and flashlight as part of his basic survival gear, especially in remote country.

of emergency supplies and equipment with you when you hunt—especially in remote areas—will help you survive should you become lost or injured. A few basic first-aid supplies and a bottle of water are also good to have along.

What should be in your emergency survival pack? First of all, stick matches, and they should be carried in a plastic bag or small, waterproof container. A thin, waterproof survival blanket, sometimes known as a "space blanket" is also a good idea. You can wrap up in it to stay warm or suspend it over tree limbs to create a waterproof shelter.

Audiovisual signaling devices should also be included in your emergency pack. A whistle or small air horn can be used to attract the attention of searchers, and a small hand mirror can be used for reflecting sunlight at a search airplane or helicopter. A small flashlight (with extra batteries) allows you to signal from ground to air at night. And don't think you can dispense with signaling devices.

If you're injured you might not be able to yell or jump, and from the air a person can look very small on the ground, if visible at all.

Another good survival tip is to never go hunting alone. But if you do decide to split up from your buddies during a hunt, always know which direction each are headed and agree upon a specific location and time to meet again. Cell phones can come in handy to keep you in touch with other hunters in your party, but don't depend on them. Cell phones may or may not work in remote areas, and cell phone batteries seem to go dead at the worst possible times, draining themselves even quicker in cold weather.

Map, Compass & GPS

Devices that can help prevent you from getting lost while hunting are a map, a compass, and a handheld GPS unit (Global Positioning System). Topographic maps are basic hunting tools that not only help keep you oriented, but they can also lead you to more game. How? By studying maps of your hunting area before you go hunting you can tell topography and ground cover types, see major landmarks such as rivers, streams, mountains, and hills, and in general get a lay of the land. Maps can also tip you off to where certain types of game animals may be found.

For instance, does a woodland narrow at a certain point into an hourglass shape? This may cause big-game animals to funnel through that area, making it a good place to put a ground blind or tree stand. Is there a major bend in a river or stream? If you're a duck or goose hunter, waterfowl may rest in the

A compass, map, and handheld GPS unit will all help you find your way around the backcountry.

backwater pool just below that bend, making it a good area to build or dig a shooting blind. Topographic maps can give fascinating insights into your hunting area. Learn to read them, and you'll not only become more familiar with where you hunt, you'll become a better hunter.

In order to use maps most effectively in the field, learn to use a compass along with them. This skill is known as orienteering, and can be a fun activity even when you're not hunting. To practice orienteering with a map and compass, choose a location off a given trail or road and see if you can walk to it using only your map and compass. You might want to try this first in an area you are familiar with, so that if you do get turned around you won't become seriously lost.

Once you find the location, try orienteering to a second location and then back to your original starting point. If you can find all three locations, you've just maneuvered yourself in a triangle and are well on your way to becoming proficient with a map and compass. The skill of orienteering could someday not only prevent you from getting lost, but could save your life or the life of another hunter, possibly your best hunting buddy.

Of the three devices mentioned for navigating hunting country—map, compass, and GPS—notice that the description of GPS units has been left for last. As a young person, you're probably used to using computers and other electronic devices, and maybe you think that handheld GPS units should have been mentioned first. After all, they are accurate, compact, and inexpensive; today you can buy a good quality, handheld GPS unit for less than $100. But the reason GPS has been left for last is that because these units are electronic they can fail. Their batteries may go dead, they may not be able to pick up a signal from satellites because of leaf cover or nearby mountains or hills, or you may drop the unit and break it. As helpful as handheld GPS units are for navigating backcountry, they should never be solely depended upon for finding your way. Learn to use a map and compass, as well as a handheld GPS unit—carrying all three with you is recommended—and your chances of ever becoming seriously lost while hunting will be greatly reduced.

What If I Get Lost?

Despite all the precautions just mentioned, if you hunt long enough, sooner or later you may still become disoriented in the woods. With any luck it will only be for a few minutes or few hours, not a few days.

It once happened to me in the wilderness mountains of Wyoming. I was returning to my tent camp along a trail when I noticed that there was no lake to my left, as there should have been. Without realizing it, I began walking faster and faster, and within a few minutes I found myself running down the mountain trail in a full-blown panic. I had to forcibly tell myself to stop, then retrace my steps. When I did, I quickly found that I had taken a wrong turn on the trail, and I was soon back at camp.

My story illustrates what can quickly happen when a hunter becomes disoriented or even completely lost. The mind slowly begins to panic until the body is running blindly through the woods, searching for something even vaguely familiar. What saved me from becoming totally lost was having a plan, then carrying out that plan.

First of all, if you find yourself disoriented in the woods, stop. Simply stop, sit down, and examine the situation. Stopping not only forces your body to rest, but your mind will rest, too, making it easier to make wise decisions. If you have water with you, take a drink; if you have some food, take a bite to eat. Forcing

Using a GPS unit is a great way to navigate in hunting country, but should not be solely relied upon because it may fail.

yourself to stop, slow down, and think is the first step in getting yourself back to where you know where you are, or getting yourself found by rescuers.

Next, if you can retrace your steps without making yourself more confused or further turned around, do so. If not, stay put. Aimlessly wandering around the woods will not only make you more disoriented, but will also make it harder for searchers to eventually find you.

First, build some kind of shelter that will protect you from rain, snow, and wind. Next, gather dry firewood, as much as you can. When you think you have enough firewood to keep a fire burning through the night, double the size of the pile. It is amazing how much wood even a small fire can consume during a long, dark, cold night. It's a good idea to gather a few green tree boughs while you're at it. Keep them near the fire, and if a search plane or helicopter flies over during the day and you have a fire going, quickly throw the green boughs on the flames. This will produce smoke, which will make your fire easier to see from the air.

The thing to remember when you're lost is that you eventually will be found. Your job is to make it easier for rescuers to find you rather than more difficult. Think, plan, then carry out your plan, and your unscheduled stay in the woods will end sooner rather than later.

SCOUTING THE LAND & KNOWING YOUR HUNT

Experienced hunters know that scouting their hunting territory well before the hunting seasons begin is critical to success. And pre-season scouting not only ups your odds of taking game, it's also fun. In the case of deer hunting, late summer or early fall is not too soon to begin scouting. Finding well-used

PRE-SEASON SCOUTING TIP

They're not cheap to purchase, but a trail camera or two can be invaluable when scouting a new area for big-game animals. If you are unfamiliar with their use, a trail camera attaches to a tree and takes a photo of whatever walks in front of it—24 hours a day. Positioning a trail camera in an area you want to hunt will soon tell you if any game is present.

deer trails helps you decide where to locate a ground blind or tree stand. As the season approaches, deer will begin making rubs and scrapes, giving yet additional clues to their whereabouts. Spring turkey hunters often begin their pre-season scouting as early as late winter, getting out at dawn to listen for turkeys gobbling and locating areas where the birds like to strut. The idea of pre-season scouting is to make yourself as familiar with your hunting area and the game animals that live there as possible. Do your homework, and chances are good that once the hunting season starts you will be going home with game when other hunters aren't.

Recovering a Big-Game Animal

Shooting a big-game animal with a bow and arrow is not the same as shooting it with a high-powered rifle bullet or shotgun slug. Bullets and slugs kill by sheer energy and knockdown power; arrows kill by cutting an animal, causing it to bleed to death. Those two aspects make approaching and recovering big-game animals after you shoot them very different.

For example, if you shoot a deer with a rifle bullet or shotgun slug and make a good hit in the heart/lung area, the animal will likely go down where it stands or very close by. But even if you make a solid heart/lung hit with an arrow, a deer could run several hundred yards before dying. The secret to recovering big-game animals when you are bowhunting is not to be in a hurry to follow the animal once you shoot. A good rule of thumb is to note the direction in which the animal runs after it's hit, then wait at least 30 minutes before following the blood trail. If you've made a less than solid hit, waiting an hour or more before following the blood trail is not too long. Having the discipline to not follow an animal's trail too soon is difficult for most new or young bowhunters, but absolutely necessary. Because if you attempt to track a big-game animal too soon, you may cause it to keep running and ultimately end up losing it.

Something else to keep in mind is that a wounded big-game animal hit by an arrow may not bleed much externally. You may actually have to get down on your hands and knees along a blood trail to see any tiny droplets of blood. But even if you don't see much blood, don't give up your search too soon. The animal could be bleeding heavily internally, and you may eventually find it, so be persistent.

The type of blood you find along a blood trail can tell you where the animal was hit. For example, if you find pink, frothy blood, the arrow likely pierced

TRACKING WOUNDED GAME ONTO PRIVATE PROPERTY

If you hunt on or near private property, there may come a time when an animal you've shot, such as a deer, runs onto property where you don't have permission to hunt. If that ever happens, what do you do? Can you legally track the deer onto the private property where you don't have permission to hunt? The answer, unfortunately, is no. You must ask permission of the landowner before crossing onto private property. This may seem unfair—to let a deer or other game animal suffer, possibly die, and not be retrieved—but the law is in place to prevent illegal trespassing. For example, some unethical hunters could hunt wherever they wanted and when asked if they had permission would simply say they were tracking a wounded game animal. The bottom line is that you need permission from the landowner to hunt anytime you are on private property. Some states even require the hunter to obtain that permission in writing.

one or both lungs and the animal will likely die soon. On the other hand, if the blood is dark red, the hit may have been farther back in the paunch, meaning the animal may not die as quickly, so you may want to give it more time before following the trail.

A trick some hunters use in following a weak blood trail is to hang a piece of white toilet paper from a bush or tree branch each time the trail changes course. That way, if you lose the trail, you can return to the pieces of paper and they will give you a general direction the animal is traveling.

If trailing a big-game animal after dark, the glow from a lantern can help blood droplets along the ground stand out. If you don't have a lantern, always make sure that you at least have a small flashlight with extra batteries in your hunting pack for tracking after dark.

Remember, too, that once legal hunting hours are over for the day, you may not carry a bow or gun with you in the field when tracking a wounded animal. Return the bow or gun to your vehicle, hunting camp, or house, then continue tracking and recover the animal. Obviously, not having a bow or gun with you could create a problem if the animal is not yet dead when you find it, so for that reason some hunters do not track animals at night. Rather, they prefer to wait until first light the next morning.

Once you come upon the downed animal, don't assume that it's dead.

Whether hunting with a gun or bow, be ready to shoot again. Many a hunter has been surprised to see that the animal he or she thought was dead gets up and runs off. Worse yet, a wounded big-game animal could decide to charge you, so always approach from the rear of the animal and be ready to make a final, killing shot if needed.

Field Care of Game

In some states and provinces, it is required by law that a hunter place a temporary tag on a big-game animal in the field after it is killed, then take that animal to an official checking station for final tagging. The reasons for

WHAT IS POACHING?

Poaching is the illegal taking of game animals. Poaching could involve any number of wildlife law violations, such as shooting animals at night by use of a spotlight, taking more than the daily bag limit of game animals, or illegally selling wildlife. If you see someone poaching or have knowledge that poaching is going on in your area, it is your responsibility as an ethical hunter to report the illegal activity to a law enforcement officer.

In most cases, the law enforcement officer you should contact about a wildlife law violation is the local wildlife officer, sometimes known as a game warden. Call the county sheriff's office to get the officer's phone number. Most U.S. states and Canadian provinces also have telephone "hotlines" that you can call and leave poaching information anonymously. Many of these programs offer cash rewards to the callers if their information results in the arrest and conviction of a poacher(s). To find out the poaching hotline telephone number in your area, check the hunting regulations brochure for your state or province.

A word of warning: If you see poaching taking place, never approach the poachers yourself, as doing so could put your safety or even your life in danger. Instead, try and gather as much information as possible about the poaching incident—license number of a vehicle, description and number of suspects, etc.—and turn that information over to law enforcement personnel. Again, it is your duty as a responsible hunter to report all poaching. Not doing so hurts your hunting opportunities, while at the same time tarnishes the image of ethical hunters in the eyes of the public.

these regulations are many. First, placing a temporary tag on a game animal in the field shows possession, identifying the hunter who killed it. When the animal is taken to an official checking station, the kill is recorded, the temporary tag is removed by the checking station attendant, and a permanent tag is put in its place.

Various measurements, such as weight or antler length, may also be taken of the animal while at the checking station. These measurements not only reveal the health or age of that particular animal, but the information is also used by wildlife biologists to determine the general health of the population of that species of game in that area.

Some states and provinces now only require that a hunter telephone in the information about their kill. He or she may also provide this information online via computer in some instances. Once a big-game animal has been officially checked, a hunter is then free to have the animal cleaned and processed. Most small-game animals are not required to be tagged and checked.

An ethical hunter has the responsibility to use the carcass of a game animal that he or she has killed for food. Game meat should never be wasted. And how game meat tastes on the table has much to do with how a game animal is handled in the field. Dirt, heat, and moisture spoil game meat. Prevent those three things from coming in contact with the animal you've killed, and the meat will taste much better when on the table.

Field dressing an animal is the first step in preparing it for the table. Field dressing is removing the entrails (intestines, heart, liver, lungs, etc.) of the animal, and is usually done soon after the animal is killed. It is particularly important to field dress big-game animals immediately. If a big-game animal is killed early in the hunting season when the weather is still warm, it may even be necessary to place a large bag of ice in the body cavity to cool down the meat after field dressing so that the carcass does not spoil before you can get it to a cooler.

Final dressing of a game animal is usually done when you get it home or back to your hunting camp, and involves removing the head, hide, feathers, hair, or fur of an animal. This is the final step in preparing the carcass for cooking. It may be illegal in some states/provinces to completely dress a game bird in the field, as doing so removes identifying marks that wildlife officers need to see to determine if the bird is a legal species or of legal sex.

AUTHOR'S AFTERWORD

It felt and sounded like a firecracker exploding in my left ear. I was knocked down, but not unconscious, and my mind immediately tried to figure out what was wrong—what was happening. At first, I thought that my shotgun had exploded. I had been turkey hunting and carrying the 12 gauge on a sling over my shoulder, and thought that maybe one of the 3-inch (7.6 cm) magnum shells in the magazine had detonated for some unexplained reason. But I had been carrying the gun over my right shoulder, so why was my left arm and the left side of my face stinging as if a thousand hornets were attacking?

I remember sitting up and seeing my camouflaged shotgun lying intact on the ground. It was then that my mind registered the terrifying and unbelievable fact: "I've been shot!"

Within seconds I could hear brush cracking about 30 yards (27.4 m) uphill from where I lay. "Help!" I yelled in a coarse voice that didn't sound quite like my own.

"Where are ya?" came a reply from up the hill.

"Down here," I said. "You shot me . . ."

A plaid-shirted hunter stepped from a downed treetop and yelled, "Where ya hit?"

"I'm hit in the head. Go get help!" I said.

(continued on p. 120)

"Where should I go?" he asked without coming closer, his voice now starting to quaver.

"There's a farmhouse over the hill. Go get help!" I repeated.

"Oh, my Gawd . . ." he said, and I could hear him running away through the woods. I could only hope that he was not leaving me for good.

It was then that the heaviest bleeding started. The leaves on the forest floor beneath my head were quickly covered with blood, and I remember thinking, "I'm bleeding too much . . . I might die here."

I said a short prayer, then took a handkerchief from my pocket and pressed it to my head. The cloth quickly filled with blood, but within a few minutes the bleeding began to subside. However, it was then that my left eye gradually began filling with blood. It's a strange feeling watching your own eyesight growing dimmer and dimmer until it's finally gone.

That hunting accident happened to me many years ago. I was hit with about 20 pellets from the other hunter's shotgun at about 30 yards (27.4 m). I still carry most of those lead-shot with me today in my left upper arm, neck, and the left side of my face. Unfortunately, after three surgeries over a period of several months, I permanently lost all sight in my left eye.

One irony of the incident was that at the time I was working as a certified hunter education instructor. I trained new instructors who in turn taught young people and other first-time shooters and hunters about gun safety. I always thought that if I hunted safely, I'd never be involved in a hunting accident. But now I was a statistic. Even though I was an experienced hunter, I paid the price for someone else's negligence, someone else's mistake. It's a day that changed my life forever.

Shooting and hunting bring with them a high level of responsibility. Are you ready to take on that responsibility? Only you and your parents can answer that. But I'm guessing that if you've read this far, you're ready. And if so, let me be the first to welcome you to the shooting sports—a grand adventure.

Here's wishing you safe shooting and hunting for a lifetime.

— W.H. "Chip" Gross

RESOURCES

SCHOLASTIC CLAY TARGET PROGRAM (SCTP)

SCTP is a program of the National Shooting Sports Foundation (NSSF) managed in partnership with numerous sponsors, agencies, and organizations, including each sport's national governing body: Amateur Trapshooting Association, National Skeet Shooting Association, National Sporting Clays Association, and USA Shooting. A popular team shotgun-shooting program, SCTP allows young people in elementary school through high school to compete on local, state, and national levels in trap, skeet, sporting clays, and the international versions of skeet and bunker trap.

· Commonly referred to as "the Little League of shooting sports," SCTP has grown phenomenally since its launch in 2000. In 2007, for example, nearly 10,000 students nationwide competed in SCTP state and national championship events, about 25 percent more than in 2006.

· The number of young women participating in SCTP has increased by more than 200 percent in the past four years, as more and more girls discover the fun of competing with and against the boys.

· Divisions in SCTP include Rookie (grades 5 and under), Intermediate (grades 6 through 8), and Junior Varsity and Varsity (grades 9 through 12).

· Championships for trap, skeet, and sporting clays are held at the World Shooting and Recreational Complex in Sparta, Illinois. The mega-competition kicks off the annual Grand American World Trapshooting

(continued on p. 122)

Championships. SCTP also partners with USA Shooting to hold the SCTP/USA Shooting Junior Olympic National Championships at the Olympic Shooting Park outside Colorado Springs, Colorado. This event includes international skeet and bunker trap, which are shot in the Olympics and at other world-level events.

This program provides young people around the country with the chance to compete as a team in the shotgun sports for state, regional, and national championships. "Getting a team started in your area can be as easy as one, two, three," said Zach Snow of the NSSF. "The first thing is to find a coach, whether it be tugging on your dad's shirt sleeve or finding someone at a local gun club or school interested in working with youths. After that, find a local gun club and see if they're willing to support your team and encourage youngsters to come out. If everyone is interested, all it takes is visiting our Web site and downloading the necessary forms."

If you or a potential coach would like to learn more about SCTP, you can request a free "Information Packet" at http://www.nssf.org/sctp. Also, if anyone is looking to gain the support of a local school or gun club, a free "Presentation Packet" includes two DVDs about the program. Contacting your SCTP state director is another way to learn more. A list of state directors is available on the SCTP Web site. "Once you have a team together, start practicing," Snow said. "And if you have other gun clubs in the area with teams, set up a local inter-club match prior to the state championship. After that, maybe we'll see you at the nationals." Visit SCTP online at: http://www.nssf.org/sctp.

NATIONAL YOUTH FIREARM & ARCHERY PROGRAMS

National Rifle Association (NRA)
Youth Hunter Education Challenge
http://www.nrahq.org/hunting/
youthed.asp

National Shooting Sports Foundation
(NSSF) Scholastic Clay Target Program
(SCTP)
http://www.nssf.org/sctp/about.cfm

National Shooting Sports Foundation
(NSSF) Scholastic Rifle Program
http://www.nssf.org/SRP/

4-H Shooting Sports Program
http://www.4-hshootingsports.org/

Boy Scouts of America
http://www.scouting.org/
HealthandSafety/GSS/gss08.asp

USA Shooting
http://www.usashooting.org/

Junior USA Shooting Team
http://www.nssf/org/JrUSA/

Civilian Marksmanship Program (CMP)
http://www.odcmp.com/

National Archery in the Schools
Program (NASP)
https://archeryintheschools.org/
activea.asp

National Field Archery Association (NFAA),
After School Archery Program (ASAP)
http://www.nfaaarchery.org/programs/
asap/asap.cfm

USA Archery Junior Olympic Archery
Development
http://www.usaarcheryjoad.org

SHOOTING, HUNTING & WILDLIFE CONSERVATION ORGANIZATIONS

U. S. Fish & Wildlife Service
Department of the Interior
1849 C Street NW
Washington, DC 20240
http://www.fws.gov

Safari Club International
4800 West Gates Pass Road
Tucson, AZ 85745-9490
http://www.safariclub.org

Ducks Unlimited, Inc.
One Waterfowl Way
Memphis, TN, 38120
http://www.ducks.org

Pheasants Forever
1783 Buerkle Circle
St Paul, MN 55110
http://www.pheasantsforever.org

National Wild Turkey Federation
P.O. Box 530
Edgefield, SC 29824
http://www.nwtf.org

Quail Unlimited
P.O. Box 610
Edgefield, SC 29824
http://www.qu.org

Rocky Mountain Elk Foundation
5705 Grant Creek
Missoula, MT 59808
http://www.rmef.org

The Ruffed Grouse Society
451 McCormick Road
Coraopolis, PA 15108
http://www.ruffedgrousesociety.org

Wildlife Forever
2700 Freeway Boulevard #1000
Brooklyn Center, MN 55430
http://www.wildlifeforever.org

International Hunter
Education Association
2727 W. 92nd Avenue, Suite 103
Federal Heights, CO 80260
http://www.ihea.com

National Shooting Sports Foundation
11 Mile Hill Road
Newtown, CT 06470
http://www.nssf.org

U. S. Sportsmen's Alliance
801 Kingsmill Parkway
Columbus, OH 43229
http://www.ussportsmen.org

National Rifle Association
11250 Waples Mill Road
Fairfax, VA 22030
http://www.nra.org

Izaak Walton League of America
707 Conservation Lane
Gaithersburg, MD 20878
http://www.iwla.org

National Field Archery Association
31407 Outer I-10
Redlands, California 92373
http://www.nfaa-archery.org

National Muzzle Loading
Rifle Association
P.O. Box 67
Friendship, IN 47021
http://www.nmlra.org

National Bowhunter
Education Foundation
P.O. Box 180757
Ft. Smith, AR 72918
http://www.nbef.org

Christian Bowhunters of America
2205 S.R. 571 West
Greenville, OH 45331-9425
http://www.christianbowhunters.org

Whitetails Unlimited, Inc.
P.O. Box 720
Sturgeon Bay, WI 54235
http://www.whitetailsunlimited.org

American Crossbow Federation
P.O. Box 251, 20 NE 9th Avenue
Glenwood, MN 56334
http://www.horizontalbowhunter.com

National Sporting Clays Association
5931 Roft Road
San Antonio, TX 78253
http://www.mynsca.com

Amateur Trapshooting
Association of America
601 W. National Road
Vandalia, OH 45377
http://www.shootata.com

National Skeet Shooting Association
5931 Roft Road
San Antonio, TX 78253
http://www.mynssa.com

USA Shooting Team
1 Olympic Plaza
Colorado Springs, CO 80909
http://www.usashooting.com

Waterfowl USA
Box 50, The Waterfowl Building
Edgefield, SC 29824
http://www.waterfowlusa.org

Civilian Marksmanship Program
P.O. Box 576
Port Clinton, OH 43452
http://www.odcmp.com

Delta Waterfowl
P.O. Box 3128
Bismarck, ND 58502
http://www.deltawaterfowl.org

PHOTO CREDITS

10-Pt. Crossbow
p. 48 (lower)

Browning Archery
p. 48 (left)

Istock
p. 1 (Lawrence Sawyer), 8, 11, 16 top),
 21 (right), 22, 24, 25, 26, 27, 29, 31,
33, 35 (lower / Ryan Howe), 76, 96
(Lawrence Sawyer), 97 (Sascha Burkard),
 107 (Al Braunworth), 109 (Ryan Howe),
 110 (top left: Onur Kocamaz; top
middle: Sven Larsen; top right: Feng
Yu; lower left: Les Cunliffe; lower right:
Craig Veitri), 111 (map / Robert Dant)

© Tes Randle Jolly
p. 23, 28, 31 (lower), 69, 74, 91, 101,
103, 105, 107 (lower)

© Lon Lauber
p. 6, 9, 10, 12, 13, 14, 15, 16 (lower), 17,
18, 19, 20, 21, 35 (top), 36, 37, 38, 40,
41, 43, 44, 46, 51, 53, 55, 57, 58, 61, 62,
63, 65, 66, 67, 71, 73, 78, 80, 81, 82, 83,
85, 86, 87, 88, 92, 93, 94, 99, 100, 108,
113

© Carol Migdalski
p. 18 (left), 73

© Tom Migdalski
p. 14, 15, 16 (lower), 17, 18 (right), 19
(right), 19, 41, 43, 71 (both), 80, 81, 82

Ragim
p. 48 (middle, right)

Thompson/Center
p. 31 (top)

Photography Contacts

10-Pt. Crossbow
330 628 9245
www.tenpointcrossbows.com

Browning Archery
520 838 2000
www.browning-archery.com

Ragim
Via Napoleonica
Forgaria nel Friuli (ud)
Italy, 33030
+39 0427 808189
www.ragim.org

Thompson/Center
603 330 5659
www.tcarms.com

INDEX

~~~~~~~~~~